YOU MUST
REMEMBER
THIS

D0963339

YOU MUST REMEMBER THIS

*Easy Tricks and Proven Tips
to Never Forget Anything, Ever Again*

Karen Dolby

Broadway Books
New York

Copyright © 2009 by Karen Dolby

All rights reserved.
Published in the United States by Broadway Books, an imprint of the
Crown Publishing Group, a division of Random House, Inc., New York.
www.crownpublishing.com

BROADWAY BOOKS and the Broadway Books colophon
are trademarks of Random House, Inc.

Originally published in Great Britain in slightly different form as
*Mrs. Dolby's Memory Magic: A Comprehensive Compendium of Tools, Tips,
and Exercises to Help You Remember Everything* by Preface Publishing,
an imprint of Random House Group, Ltd., London, in 2009.

Library of Congress Cataloging-in-Publication Data
Dolby, Karen.
[Mrs. Dolby's memory magic]
You must remember this : easy tricks and proven tips to never forget
anything, ever again / Karen Dolby. — 1st U.S. ed.
p.   cm.
1. Mnemonics. I. Title.
BF385.D65 2010
153.1'4—dc22
2010022626

ISBN 978-0-307-71625-5

Printed in the United States of America

Design by Peter Ward

1 3 5 7 9 10 8 6 4 2

First U.S. Edition

For Trevor, George, and Freya

CONTENTS

~⊷ CONTENTS ⊶~

INTRODUCTION

"Study without desire spoils the memory, and it retains nothing that it takes in."

L EONARDO DA V INCI

How often have you heard the complaints "I've got a terrible memory," "My brain's like a sieve," or "I simply forget everything"? At some point in our busy lives, most of us wish we had a better memory. But it's not that you have a bad memory, it's simply that you are not using it efficiently.

From the moment we are born, and perhaps even before that, our brain takes in information that it processes, encodes, and then stores away. When people complain that they have a bad memory, what they are really saying is that they have trouble retrieving their memories—all the facts and information are safely locked in the brain; the problem is access. It's easy to upgrade the memory on a computer—just find a compatible system. What most people don't realize is that it's just as simple to do the same for your brain. All it takes is a little know-how and training.

Winston Churchill famously made a point of never memorizing his speeches verbatim after one disastrous occasion when his mind went completely blank. What he did instead was to memorize what he wanted to say—the key points—along with a few suitably elegant, clever, or stirring phrases. Daniel Tammet, who won worldwide acclaim for his memoir of life with autistic savant syndrome, believes that the differences between savant and nonsavant minds are exaggerated and that his astonishing feats of memory are the result of complex associative ways of thinking that we can all aspire to.

Many of the greatest actors, linguists, and speech makers don't have naturally brilliant memories; what they do have is a range of memory systems and mnemonic tools to help them. You simply need to find the techniques and tricks that work for you.

Mnemonics help your memory function more efficiently by using a number of different devices, including rhymes, sentences, diagrams, acronyms, and rules to easily retrieve names, dates, lists, facts, and figures. The word comes from the Greek *mneme,* meaning "memory," and *mnemon,* meaning "mindful." Mnemosyne was the ancient Greek goddess of memory, mother of the Muses.

Mnemonics work because they force your mind to really pay attention to what you're learning. So often we instantly forget someone's name when first introduced simply because we didn't listen properly, our mind already thinking of our next comment. Mnemonics also help to organize the information, which again makes it easier to retrieve later. Research shows that mental capacity to remember can be vastly increased by simply breaking numbers or letters into groups. This breakdown is usually called chunking and works particularly well if the chunks can be made memorable. The ideal length for chunking letters and numbers is three, which explains the way in which most telephone numbers are broken up.

Many mnemonics are so much a part of everyday use that we often don't realize we are using a memory device. For instance, "Spring forward, fall back" reminds us the clocks go forward one hour in spring and back in autumn, and a rhyme we all learned in school helps us to remember the number of days in each month:

> Thirty days hath September,
> April, June, and November,
> All the rest have thirty-one,
> Except February alone,
> Which has twenty-eight days clear,
> And twenty-nine in each leap year.

It's interesting that most people have no difficulty reciting this absolutely correctly, because other thirty-one-day months could easily be substituted for the four thirty-day months and the rhyme would still work.

In this book I will be reminding you of all the mnemonics you've ever learned and possibly forgotten, along with plenty of new ones. There are also clear explanations of the different memory systems used by memory masters. I have tried to be as comprehensive and wide-ranging as possible, but the topics covered are a subjective list. They are all areas that I remember from childhood and others that have interested me since. Sometimes several mnemonics are suggested for the same thing. This is because different ideas appeal to different people and for a mnemonic to work well it has to mean something. Whether it is funny or just appeals, there needs to be a connection; it has to spark an image and emotional response in order to be memorable.

One of the most important things I have learned while researching this book is that for most people there is no such thing as a good or bad memory. Putting aside all the clever memory systems and thousands of punchy mnemonics, the key is really effort and interest. People with so-called good memories usually work at it: they practice and take time to learn and improve. But while there are no instant shortcuts, this does mean that a better memory is a real possibility for everyone.

And there are definite benefits. There's a growing body of evidence suggesting that mental training in a subject that interests you improves not only memory but cognitive functioning. To quote the director of the Memory Clinic at Johns Hopkins, Barry Gordon, "If you want to improve your mental functioning, pick something you are interested in and work at it."

> *"Nothing fixes a thing so intensely in the memory as the wish to forget it."*
>
> MICHEL DE MONTAIGNE

YOU MUST REMEMBER THIS

THE LINK AND STORY METHOD— REMEMBERING A SIMPLE LIST

The Link method is probably one of the most basic mnemonic techniques. It is easy to understand and worth mastering before moving on to some of the other memory techniques. At its most simple it works by linking words together using images, but before I explain it fully, take a moment to test yourself. Study the following list of random words—really take the time to try to remember them—then turn the book over and write down the words in order.

Tepee
Fountain
Fish
Marathon
Grapes
Broom
Clock
Chocolate
Shower
Boat

How far did you get? And if asked to write the same list backward or in ten minutes' time, how many words would you remember then? But if you assign each word an image and then link it to the next, you will find you can do much better with a little practice.

The key to mastering this technique is to make each image as vivid and unusual as possible. Each should interact or link with the next; it won't work simply to imagine one standing beside another. For instance, the fountain should actually be erupting from the top of the tepee, which instead of fabric could be carved from stone with strange carvings on the sides.

The important thing is that the image should mean something to you. It could be personal or just something that amuses or even disgusts you. Laughter is always helpful for keeping something in mind, and repellent ideas are likewise hard to forget.

So bearing all this in mind, the pictures for the list could go something like this:

A carved stone Tepee erupts into a Fountain that is flowing with giant Fish with gnashing teeth. When they hit the ground the Fish grow legs and run a Marathon, snapping at the heels of the other runners. The other runners appear to be Grapes, purple, bloated and overripe, oozing puslike juice. A giant cartoon Broom appears from the sky and sweeps the Grapes away. The Broom has a long handle and swings rhythmically to and fro because it is the pendulum of a huge sun Clock. The Clock darkens because it is made of Chocolate melting in the heat, the numbers and hands lengthening and distorting as it begins to drip. The Chocolate drips are now gushing from a Shower, which is attached to a bathtub Boat bobbing up and down; inside a rower bails frantically as chocolate cascades from the Shower filling his bath Boat.

Read this carefully, picturing each cameo as you go, then turn the book over and try writing out the list again. Let each image lead you effortlessly on to the next. It's surprising how much easier it is to remember everything.

This was only a very short list, but try this technique next time you go shopping. By linking each item on your list with an entertaining image, you'll find yourself becoming ever more ingenious, and you can develop the Link method further by weaving a story around your pictures. Be creative and let your imagination run wild, and don't be afraid to add sound effects or vibrant colors if these work well for you.

The Link method is not only useful for remembering lists, it can also be used to remind yourself to do something. For instance, if you promised to call a friend before supper, imagine their face on the stove smiling up at you, mouthing the words "Call me," or picture them as the wooden spoon you use to stir your soup.

Even speeches can be learned by representing each of the points you need to make by clear images, vividly linked together. Once you are practiced in the technique, you will be able to do away with notes altogether and appear far more relaxed and confident. In the same way you can learn poems or your part in a play or apply the method to help with studying for exams, recalling events, theories, or case studies.

WHERE MEMORIES ARE STORED
IN THE BRAIN

The hippocampus is one of the main parts of the brain involved in the forming, sorting, and storing of memories. Not only does the hippocampus store memories, it also connects them with other related memories, giving meaning and context.

The hippocampus is located in the medial temporal lobe of the brain. Early scientists likened the shape to a ram's horn or sea horse, and the sixteenth-century anatomist Julius Caesar Arazi gave the structure its Greek name meaning "sea horse." Together with the adjacent amygdala, the hippocampus forms the central axis of the limbic system, the emotion system of the brain, in charge of the transfer of information into memory.

LANGUAGE

�֍

"Memory feeds imagination."
AMY TAN

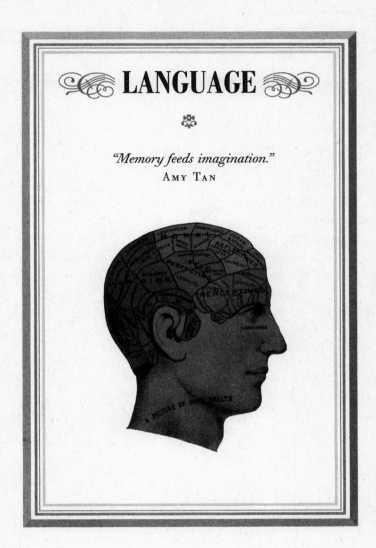

The first mnemonics I ever learned are all connected with learning to read and write, and I suspect I am not unusual in this. In fact so ingrained in my memory are these simple rhymes, chants, and catchphrases that I don't even remember being taught them. They simply spring to mind automatically, particularly for spellings.

SPELLING BEE

One of the many peculiarities of the English language is the set of rules on spelling, which always apply, except when they don't. There are several rhyming phrases taught to schoolchildren from time immemorial to help them recall certain of these rules.

Perhaps the most common is:
"I" before "E" except after "C."

Although sadly this rule does not always apply, which has led to:
"I" before "E" except after "C"
Though "weird" is just "weird."

(And so incidentally are *Budweiser, feisty, forfeit, heifer, height,* heirloom, kaleidoscope, leisure, seismic, seize, and weir, to list but a few.)

The other main exceptions to the rule are words where "EI" is pronounced as "A," for instance, abseil, reign, and feign, which have prompted this version:

"I" before "E" except after "C"
Or when sounded like "A" as in neighbor and weigh.

CATCHPHRASES/WORDPLAY

Clever or rhythmic phrases can also help with spelling.
To spell *cemetery* with three "Es," remember:
She cried, "E . . . e . . . e!" as she ran past the cemetery.

Friend or *freind*?
You always need friends to the end.

Argument or *arguement*?
Argue lost an "E" in an argument.

To recall the number of "Cs" in *necessary* and *success:*
Only one "C" is necessary, but you need two "Cs" for success.

There are various chants that work for *Mississippi:*
· *Say to yourself, "M-I-S, S-I-S, S-I-P, P-I." Try it out loud; there is a natural rhythm that begins to make sense the more you say it.*
· *Or you may prefer "Mrs. M, Mrs. I, Mrs. SSI, Mrs. SSI, Mrs. PPI."*

In a similar vein, Roald Dahl spelled out *difficulty* in *Matilda:* "*Mrs. D, Mrs. I, Mrs. F F I, Mrs. C, Mrs. U, Mrs. L T Y.*"

To spell *separate,* use this story:
There was once a farmer named Sep, and when his wife saw a rat she yelled, "Sep, a rat! E!!!"

There are two options for *together:*
We went to get her.
Or you may prefer:
Remember if you get her you'll be together.

Ascertain
When you ascertain a fact, always be As Certain as you possibly can.

Bookkeeper
Triple compound: oo kk ee.

Potassium
Remember one tea but two sugars.

Slaughter (which always makes me smile)
Slaughter is simply Laughter with an "S" at the beginning.

Innocent
IN NO CENTury is murder an innocent crime.

SPELLING ACRONYMS

Take the initial letter of each word in a memorable sentence to correctly spell words that people often find tricky.

Mnemonics
> *Mnemonics Now Erase Man's Oldest Nemesis: Insufficient Cerebral Storage.*

Necessary
> *Never Eat Chips; Eat Salad Sandwiches And Remain Young.*

Rhythm
> *Rhythm Has Your Two Hips Moving.*

Because
> *Big Elephants Can Always Understand Small Elephants.*

Arithmetic
> *A Rat In The House Might Eat The Ice Cream.*

Wednesday
> *WE Do Not Eat Soup DAY, or more simply and certainly the way I always think of the word, just sound out Wed-nes-day.*

Geography
> *General Eisenhower's Old Grandfather Rode A Pig Home Yesterday.*

Ocean
> *Only Cats' Eyes Are Narrow.*

COMMON CONFUSIONS

Homophones are words that sound the same (or similar) but have different spellings and meanings.

Affect the effect
> *The word* raven *can help you remember when to use* affect *and when* effect *is the correct choice.*

> R *emember*
> A *ffect*
> V *erb*
> E *ffect*
> N *oun*

Desert desserts
> *Remember a desert is sandy with only one "S," while desserts have two "Ss" like sweet stuff, strawberry shortcake, and two scoops of ice cream. If you eat too many desserts, you may feel stressed, which helpfully is simply* desserts *spelled backward.*

Hear, here
> *You hear with your ear.*

Stationary stationery
> *To be sure of the difference, remember that a station stAnds still—it's stationAry—and a stationEr sElls stationEry.*

Sculpture and sculptor
> *A sculptor works with stone to create a sculPTURE, which is a
> kind of PicTURE.*

The principles of principals
> *Your princiPAL is your PAL (in a perfect world), while the ruLEs
> he lives by can be called principLEs and both end in LE.*

There and They're
> *There is a place just like here.*
> *They're is when they want to say they are.*

COORDINATING CONJUNCTIONS

BOAF SYN

Is an acronym for:
> But
> Or
> And
> For
> So
> Yet
> Nor

ONOMATOPOEIA

A strange-looking word that comes from two Greek words meaning "name" and "I make." An onomatopoeia sounds like the thing it is describing, for instance, buzz, squelch, cuckoo (which hasn't changed from its Anglo-Saxon origins), Ping-Pong, swish, and cartoon expletives such as thwack, wham, biff, and pow.

Onomatopoeias are sometimes called literary mnemonics and are popular devices in advertising because they automatically remind you of exactly what they are describing: just think of the slogan "Snap, crackle and pop" for Rice Krispies or "Clunk, click every trip" in the campaign started in the 1970s prompting everyone to fasten their seat belts.

There are onomatopoeias in every language, from *tuxtux,* which is the Latin equivalent of "bam" or "whack," to *dodidoki* to describe in Japanese a beating heart. They are also used as mnemonics in music, for example, in kuchi shoga, the Japanese system for pronouncing drum sounds.

To remember how to correctly spell onomatopoeia, sound out the first part—On O Mato—then use the acronym Points Of Exaggeration In Art for the last bit.

FIGURES OF SPEECH

Most People Sing In Harmony usefully recalls:
Metaphor, Personification, Simile, Irony, Hyperbole.

SPLIT INFINITIVES

This describes a sentence where an adverb is placed between the infinitive marker *to* and the verb itself. Perhaps the easiest way to remember is simply to recall possibly the most famous example of all time from the opening sequence of *Star Trek:*

"*To boldly go* where no man has gone before."

Although traditional grammar views splitting the infinitive as incorrect, particularly in formal written English, the rule is gradually disappearing. Many writers feel that the most natural position for the adverb is often between *to* and the verb—for example: "George promised to really try this time"—and that avoiding the split simply results in clumsier sentences.

PALINDROMES

A palindrome is a word or phrase that reads the same forward and backward, for example, the name Anna and words such as *deified* and *reviver.* Numbers and sequences can also be palindromes.

The discovery of graffiti at Herculaneum depicting a palindromic word square shows that palindromes date back to at least the first century, when Herculaneum was engulfed by a pyroclastic mudflow following the eruption of Vesuvius in AD 79.

S	A	T	O	R
A	R	E	P	O
T	E	N	E	T
O	P	E	R	A
R	O	T	A	S

The word *arepo* is unknown to translators, which makes the meaning debatable. It is sometimes translated as "The sower Arepo holds the wheels at work," but it may also have been a secret Christian sign, with *tenet* (from *tenere*, meaning "to hold") forming a cross.

USEFUL TERMS TO REMEMBER/LANGUAGE AND GRAMMAR

Every name is called a Noun
Like field and fountain, street and town.

In place of a noun the Pronoun stands
For he, she, and it can clap their hands.

An Adjective describes a thing
Like magic wand and feathered wing.

The Verb means action, something done
To read, to write, to walk, to run.

How things are done, the Adverbs tell
Like quickly, slowly, badly, well.

A Preposition shows relation
As in the street, or at the station.

Conjunctions join in different ways
Sentences, words, or thought and phrase.

An Interjection suggests surprise
As Oh! How splendid! Oh my! You're wise!

Through poetry we learn how each
Makes up the different parts of speech.

Prefixes

A prefix is a small group of letters, which often come from Greek or Latin, that are added to the beginning of a word to alter its meaning: for example, *dis*appear, *mis*inform, *extra*ordinary.

Suffixes

Suffixes are also added to words to change their function or meaning but are attached to the end rather than the beginning. For example, *ly* turns an adjective into an adverb: the adjectives *wild* and *careful* become the adverbs *wildly* and *care-*

fully; or the addition of *man* to *work* (*workman*) or *wright* to *play* to create *playwright.*

To remember the difference between the two, just think of the word *previous* for prefix or simply that "P" comes before "S" in the alphabet.

ELEMENTS OF STORIES

Very Many Pupils Come To School reminds us to include:
Viewpoint, Mood, Plot, Characters, Theme, Setting.

LITERARY GENRES

Just remember "3Ps":
Plays, Poetry, Prose.

Practice the Link and Story Method (page 3), or one of the other memory systems described later, to learn this simple list of words.

THE TEN MOST COMMONLY USED WORDS IN THE ENGLISH LANGUAGE

There are various definitive lists, all different. The following list was compiled by Oxford Online in association with the

Oxford English Dictionary, which seems a reliable source to consult.

1	the	6	a
2	be	7	in
3	to	8	that
4	of	9	have
5	and	10	I

LITERATURE

"If any one faculty of our nature may be called more wonderful than the rest, I do think it is memory. There seems something more speakingly incomprehensible in the powers, the failures, the inequalities of memory, than in any other of our intelligences. The memory is sometimes so retentive, so serviceable, so obedient; at others, so bewildered and so weak; and at others again, so tyrannic, so beyond control! We are, to be sure, a miracle every way; but our powers of recollecting and of forgetting do seem peculiarly past finding out."

JANE AUSTEN,
Mansfield Park

JANE AUSTEN
(December 16, 1775–July 18, 1817)

Jane Austen is one of the most famous and beloved of English novelists. Her books provide a wonderful insight into the lives of the middle and upper classes, particularly women, in the early nineteenth century. Renowned for their wit and social observation, her novels were originally published anonymously, simply stating they were by "A Lady." Since 1833, when they were first published in a collected edition, they have never been out of print. Though she was little known during her short lifetime, in 1869 Jane's nephew, James Edward Austen-Leigh, published *A Memoir of Jane Austen*, which introduced her to a wider audience and rekindled interest. From that time her worldwide fan base of Janeites has grown steadily, reflected in numerous films and TV adaptations of her life and works.

How to Remember Her Published Novels

Sense and Sensibility, *1811*
Pride and Prejudice, *1813*
Mansfield Park, *1814*
Emma, *1816*

Northanger Abbey
Persuasion

} *published posthumously in 1818*

a Sense of Pride Makes Emma Notably Perky.

Or you may prefer:

Senseless Pride Makes Everyone Notoriously Prickly.

As well as her novels, Jane Austen wrote three unfinished works of fiction: *Lady Susan*, 1794 and 1805; *The Watsons*, 1804; and *Sanditon*, 1817. She also wrote three volumes of juvenilia begun while still in her teens: *Sir Charles Grandison*, 1793 and 1800; *Plan of a Novel*, 1815; and poems and prayers. Of an estimated 3,000 letters, only about 160 survive. After her death, Jane's sister, Cassandra, burned many and censored others. More were later destroyed by the family of her brother, Admiral Francis Austen.

WILLIAM SHAKESPEARE
(April 23, 1564–April 23, 1616)

It's one thing to devise a simple mnemonic acronym for the novels of Jane Austen, but what if you want to remember everything that Shakespeare wrote?

One option is to apply one of the memory systems; for instance, the Link system might help if you can visualize an image for each play (there are thirty-seven in case you're wondering, or thirty-eight if you accept *The Two Noble Kinsmen*; and then of course there are the sonnets and poems). Star-crossed lovers obviously for *Romeo and Juliet*; spirits, a magician, and a monstrous creature whirling above a storm-lashed sea in *The Tempest;* Shakespeare's caricature of a hunchbacked loathsome king in *Richard III,* and so on. You don't have to know the play to think of an image; just let the wording of the title suggest something you will find memorable, however unconnected with Shakespeare.

It also helps to break down the lists as much as possible, and alphabetizing also always helps me to order things in my mind.

And so we have:

Comedies

All's Well That Ends Well

As You Like It

The Comedy of Errors

Love's Labors Lost

Measure for Measure

The Merchant of Venice

The Merry Wives of Windsor

A Midsummer Night's Dream

Much Ado About Nothing

Pericles, Prince of Tyre

The Taming of the Shrew

The Tempest

Twelfth Night

The Two Gentlemen of Verona

The Two Noble Kinsmen *(attributed to Shakespeare and John Fletcher)*

A Winter's Tale

Histories

Henry IV, Part 1
Henry IV, Part 2
Henry V
Henry VI, Part 1
Henry VI, Part 2
Henry VI, Part 3
Henry VIII
King John
Richard II
Richard III

Tragedies

Antony and Cleopatra
Coriolanus
Cymbeline
Hamlet
Julius Caesar
King Lear
Macbeth
Othello
Romeo and Juliet
Timon of Athens
Titus Andronicus
Troilus and Cressida
(*Cymbeline* and *Troilus and Cressida* are sometimes labeled
"problem plays" by critics and are not always regarded as
tragedies because they do not conform strictly to the rules of

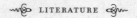

tragedy. Partly for this reason, sometimes a fourth category of plays labeled "romance" is introduced.)

Poetry

Sonnets
A Lover's Complaint
The Rape of Lucrece
Venus and Adonis
Funeral Elegy

MEMORIZING

When you try to fix anything in your memory, it is always useful to write it down and then compare it with the original. After you have checked and made any corrections, try again after an hour, then a day, a week, and at regular intervals.

Shakespeare's Life

William Shakespeare is regarded by many as the greatest playwright of all time, yet very little is known for certain of his life. We know he was born in Stratford-upon-Avon in 1564 and died, aged fifty-two, in 1616 on his birthday, April 23 (also rather appropriately for such a notable Englishman, St. George's Day). He married Anne Hathaway in 1582 at the age of eighteen, and they had three children, Susanna and the twins,

Hamnet and Judith. At some point between 1585 and 1592 he moved to London without his family to forge his career as an actor and writer. He was a prominent member of the theatre company the Chamberlain's Men, later called the King's Men, which built and occupied the Globe Theatre on the river Thames from 1599. Over the course of his career, Shakespeare became the most popular playwright in England and was patronized by both Queen Elizabeth I and King James I.

Although also celebrated for his sonnets, "the play's the thing!" (*Hamlet*, act II, scene II), and rarely a minute goes past without one of his plays being performed somewhere in the world, whether on a school or a professional stage.

LINES TO REMEMBER

There is nothing quite so satisfying for testing your memory as knowing a few poems or lines of Shakespeare by heart. Once learned they tend to stick. There are lines and quotations I learned at school that I mentally revisit on occasion almost to check that they are still there and to reassure me my memory is still working. They are also useful as party tricks, in times of boredom or stress, and even to recite aloud in the darkness while trying to coax a determinedly wide-awake small child to sleep. I found I could choose the lines; the important thing was that they flowed mellifluously and encouraged the afore-mentioned insomniac to drift sweetly to sleep "perchance to dream."

The choice of passage should be your own. Choose something you like, for whatever reason. It should be a passage you find memorable or that speaks to you. These are among my favorites:

Jacques' speech on the seven ages of man:

All the world's a stage,
And all the men and women merely players:
They have their exits and their entrances;
And one man in his time plays many parts,
His acts being seven ages. At first the infant,
Mewling and puking in the nurse's arms.
And then the whining school-boy, with his satchel,
And shining morning face, creeping like snail
Unwillingly to school. And then the lover,
Sighing like furnace, with a woeful ballad
Made to his mistress' eyebrow. Then a soldier,
Full of strange oaths, and bearded like the pard,
Jealous in honor, sudden and quick in quarrel,
Seeking the bubble reputation
Even in the cannon's mouth. And then the justice,
In fair round belly with good capon lined,
With eyes severe, and beard of formal cut,
Full of wise saws and modern instances;
And so he plays his part. The sixth age shifts
Into the lean and slipper'd pantaloon,
With spectacles on nose and pouch on side,
His youthful hose well saved, a world too wide
For his shrunk shank; and his big manly voice,

Turning again toward childish treble, pipes
And whistles in his sound. Last scene of all,
That ends this strange eventful history,
Is second childishness and mere oblivion,
Sans teeth, sans eyes, sans taste, sans every thing.

As You Like It, act II, scene VII, c. 1599

Hamlet's famous musings on the futility of life and mortality, quoted to poignant effect by Richard E. Grant in the final scene of the film *Withnail and I*:

I have of late, but wherefore I know not, lost all my
mirth, foregone all custom of exercises; and indeed it
goes so heavily with my disposition that this goodly
frame, the earth, seems to me a sterile promontory;
this most excellent canopy, the air, look you, this brave
o'erhanging firmament, this majestical roof fretted
with golden fire, why, it appears no other thing to me
than a foul and pestilent congregation of vapours.
What a piece of work is a man! how noble in reason!
how infinite in faculty! in form and moving how
express and admirable! in action how like an angel! in
apprehension how like a god! the beauty of the world!
the paragon of animals! And yet, to me, what is this
quintessence of dust? Man delights not me; no, nor
women neither . . .

Hamlet, act II, scene II, c. 1600

And Enobarbus says of "that lass unparalled," Cleopatra:

> Age cannot wither her, nor custom stale
> Her infinite variety; other women cloy
> The appetites they feed, but she makes hungry
> Where most she satisfies . . .
>
> *Antony and Cleopatra*, act II, scene II, c. 1607

EMILY DICKINSON
(December 10, 1830–May 15, 1886)

Emily Dickinson was born in Massachusetts and rarely left her family home in Amherst, choosing to withdraw into a life of solitude. She was a prolific writer, particularly from the late 1850s. In 1862 alone she wrote 366 poems. However, the majority were not published until after her death, the full texts appearing only in 1955, and of the few published during her lifetime, most were badly altered by editors or printers. Critical acclaim gained momentum, and she is now considered to be a major American poet. Her poems are unusual for her time, as she usually wrote short lines, rarely more than twelve, often without title and with unconventional punctuation.

> This is my letter to the World
> That never wrote to Me—
> The simple News that Nature told—
> With tender Majesty

Her Message is committed
To Hands I cannot see—
For love of Her—Sweet—countrymen—
Judge tenderly—of Me

EDGAR ALLAN POE
(January 19, 1809–October 7, 1849)

Edgar Allan Poe was one of the nineteenth-century pioneers of American literature and another of the "great irrepressible solitaries," as Saul Bellow labeled him. Poe is probably best known for his macabre mystery stories and is regarded as the inventor of detective fiction, also working as an editor and literary critic as well as writing poetry. He died at the young age of forty, and there was wide speculation as to the cause, including suicide, alcohol, drugs, rabies, heart failure, and tuberculosis.

For a real memory challenge, you could set yourself to memorizing "The Raven." If you prefer something less lengthy, try "A Dream Within a Dream."

The Raven

Once upon a midnight dreary, while I pondered weak and
   weary,
Over many a quaint and curious volume of forgotten lore,
While I nodded, nearly napping, suddenly there came a
   tapping,

As of some one gently rapping, rapping at my chamber door.
"'Tis some visitor," I muttered, "tapping at my chamber
    door—
Only this, and nothing more."

Ah, distinctly I remember it was in the bleak December,
And each separate dying ember wrought its ghost upon the
    floor.
Eagerly I wished the morrow;—vainly I had sought to borrow
From my books surcease of sorrow—sorrow for the lost
    Lenore—
For the rare and radiant maiden whom the angels named
    Lenore—
Nameless here for evermore.

And the silken sad uncertain rustling of each purple curtain
Thrilled me—filled me with fantastic terrors never felt
    before;
So that now, to still the beating of my heart, I stood
    repeating
"'Tis some visitor entreating entrance at my chamber door—
Some late visitor entreating entrance at my chamber door;—
This it is, and nothing more."

Presently my soul grew stronger; hesitating then no longer,
"Sir," said I, "or Madam, truly your forgiveness I implore;
But the fact is I was napping, and so gently you came
    rapping,
And so faintly you came tapping, tapping at my chamber door,

That I scarce was sure I heard you"—here I opened wide the
    door;—
Darkness there, and nothing more.

Deep into that darkness peering, long I stood there
    wondering, fearing,
Doubting, dreaming dreams no mortal ever dared to dream
    before
But the silence was unbroken, and the darkness gave no token,
And the only word there spoken was the whispered word,
    "Lenore!"
This I whispered, and an echo murmured back the word,
    "Lenore!"
Merely this and nothing more.

Back into the chamber turning, all my soul within me
    burning,
Soon again I heard a tapping somewhat louder than before.
"Surely," said I, "surely that is something at my window
    lattice;
Let me see then, what thereat is, and this mystery explore—
Let my heart be still a moment and this mystery explore;—
'Tis the wind and nothing more!"

Open here I flung the shutter, when, with many a flirt and
    flutter,
In there stepped a stately raven of the saintly days of yore.
Not the least obeisance made he; not a minute stopped or
    stayed he;

But, with mien of lord or lady, perched above my chamber
    door—
Perched upon a bust of Pallas just above my chamber door—
Perched, and sat, and nothing more.

Then this ebony bird beguiling my sad fancy into smiling,
By the grave and stern decorum of the countenance it wore,
"Though thy crest be shorn and shaven, thou," I said, "art
    sure no craven.
Ghastly grim and ancient raven wandering from the nightly
    shore—
Tell me what thy lordly name is on the Night's Plutonian
    shore!"
Quoth the raven, "Nevermore."

Much I marvelled this ungainly fowl to hear discourse so
    plainly,
Though its answer little meaning—little relevancy bore;
For we cannot help agreeing that no living human being
Ever yet was blessed with seeing bird above his chamber
    door—
Bird or beast above the sculptured bust above his chamber
    door,
With such name as "Nevermore."

But the raven, sitting lonely on the placid bust, spoke only,
That one word, as if his soul in that one word he did outpour.
Nothing further then he uttered—not a feather then he
    fluttered—

Till I scarcely more than muttered "Other friends have flown
    before—
On the morrow he will leave me, as my hopes have flown
    before."
Then the bird said, "Nevermore."

Startled at the stillness broken by reply so aptly spoken,
"Doubtless," said I, "what it utters is its only stock and
    store,
Caught from some unhappy master whom unmerciful
    disaster
Followed fast and followed faster till his songs one burden
    bore—
Till the dirges of his hope that melancholy burden bore
Of 'Never-nevermore.'"

But the raven still beguiling all my sad soul into smiling,
Straight I wheeled a cushioned seat in front of bird and bust
    and door;
Then, upon the velvet sinking, I betook myself to linking
Fancy unto fancy, thinking what this ominous bird of yore—
What this grim, ungainly, ghastly, gaunt, and ominous bird of
    yore
Meant in croaking "Nevermore."

This I sat engaged in guessing, but no syllable expressing
To the fowl whose fiery eyes now burned into my bosom's
    core;
This and more I sat divining, with my head at ease reclining

On the cushion's velvet lining that the lamp-light gloated o'er,
But whose velvet violet lining with the lamp-light gloating o'er,
She shall press, ah, nevermore!

Then, methought, the air grew denser, perfumed from an
    unseen censer
Swung by Seraphim whose foot-falls tinkled on the tufted
    floor.
"Wretch," I cried, "thy God hath lent thee—by these angels he
    has sent thee
Respite—respite and nepenthe from thy memories of Lenore!
Quaff, oh quaff this kind nepenthe, and forget this lost
    Lenore!"
Quoth the raven, "Nevermore."

"Prophet!" said I, "thing of evil!—prophet still, if bird or
    devil!—
Whether tempter sent, or whether tempest tossed thee here
    ashore,
Desolate yet all undaunted, on this desert land enchanted—
On this home by horror haunted—tell me truly, I implore—
Is there—*is* there balm in Gilead?—tell me—tell me, I
    implore!'
Quoth the raven, "Nevermore."

"Prophet!" said I, "thing of evil!—prophet still, if bird or
    devil!
By that Heaven that bends above us—by that God we both
    adore—

Tell this soul with sorrow laden if, within the distant Aidenn,
It shall clasp a sainted maiden whom the angels named
    Lenore—
Clasp a rare and radiant maiden, whom the angels named
    Lenore?"
Quoth the raven, "Nevermore."

"Be that word our sign of parting, bird or fiend!" I shrieked
    upstarting—
"Get thee back into the tempest and the Night's Plutonian
    shore!
Leave no black plume as a token of that lie thy soul hath
    spoken!
Leave my loneliness unbroken!—quit the bust above my door!
Take thy beak from out my heart, and take thy form from off
    my door!"
Quoth the raven, "Nevermore."

And the raven, never flitting, still is sitting, still is sitting
On the pallid bust of Pallas just above my chamber door;
And his eyes have all the seeming of a demon's that is
    dreaming,
And the lamp-light o'er him streaming throws his shadow on
    the floor;
And my soul from out that shadow that lies floating on the
    floor
Shall be lifted—nevermore!

A Dream Within a Dream

Take this kiss upon the brow!
And, in parting from you now,
Thus much let me avow—
You are not wrong, who deem
That my days have been a dream:
Yet if hope has flown away
In a night, or in a day,
In a vision, or in none,
Is it therefore the less *gone*?
All that we see or seem
Is but a dream within a dream.

I stand amid the roar
Of a surf-tormented shore,
And I hold within my hand
Grains of the golden sand—
How few! yet how they creep
Through my fingers to the deep,
While I weep—while I weep!
O God! can I not grasp
Them with a tighter clasp?
O God! can I not save
One from the pitiless wave?
Is *all* that we see or seem
But a dream within a dream?

CHURCHILL'S MEMORY

Everyone remembers Churchill as a great orator, never at a loss for words, and with a wealth of quotations from poetry and literature at his disposal. But what many do not realize is that this did not come naturally; it took him years of practice and hard work.

As a boy, Winston Churchill suffered from a speech impediment, and yet in his first year at Harrow School, he won a contest reciting 1,300 lines of poetry from memory. He liked words and was determined; he simply persevered until he overcame the impediment.

During World War II he wrote and delivered speeches that defined key moments in British and world history. Again he studied and practiced.

His private secretary, John Colville, calculated that Churchill devoted one hour of preparation for every minute of delivery time. He also used every moment. There are stories of his shaving with poems attached to the bathroom mirror so that even those few minutes every day could be purposeful.

HOW TO LEARN A FOREIGN LANGUAGE

"Grasp the subject, the words will follow."

CATO THE ELDER

In *Use Your Memory*, Tony Buzan explains that a mere one hundred words make up about 50 percent of the total number of words used in an average conversation. It follows that by learning this basic one hundred you will vastly improve your ability to speak another language. Obviously, you would also need to check extra vocabulary but learning one hundred foreign words seems an easily achievable target for most people.

As with "The Ten Most Commonly Used Words in the English Language" (see page 19), there is some dispute about exactly which words are the most commonly used in French, but Buzan suggests these as the basic one hundred:

1. A *Un/une*	5. Almost *Presque*	9. Because *Parce que*
2. After *Après*	6. Also *Aussi*	10. Before *Avant*
3. Again *Encore*	7. Always *Toujours*	11. Big *Grand*
4. All *Chacun des*	8. And *Et*	12. But *Mais*

13. I can
Je peux

14. I come
Je viens

15. Either/or
L'un ou l'autre

16. I find
Je trouve

17. First
Premier

18. For
Pour

19. Friend
L'ami

20. From
De

21. I go
Je vais

22. Good
Bon

23. Goodbye
Au revoir

24. Happy
Heureux

25. I have
J'ai

26. He
Il

27. Hello
Bonjour

28. Here
Ici

29. How
Comment

30. I
Je

31. I am
Je suis

32. If
Si

33. In
Dans

34. I know
Je sais

35. Last
Dernier

36. I like
J'aime

37. Little
Petit

38. Love
L'amour

39. I make
Je fais

40. Many
Beaucoup de

41. One
Un/une

42. More
Plus

43. Most
La plupart de

44. Much
Beaucoup

45. My
Mon, ma, mes

46. New
Nouveau

47. No
Non

48. Not
Pas

49. Now
Maintenant

50. Of
De

51. Often
Souvent

52. On
Sur

53. Only
Seulement

54. Or
Ou

55. Other
Autre

56. Our
Notre/nos

57. Out
Dehors

58. Over
Plus de

59. People
Les gens

60. Place
L'endroit

61. Please
S'il vous plaît

62. The same
Le même

63. I see
Je vois

64. She
Elle

65. So
Alors
(So much)
Tellement

66. Some
Quelques

67. Sometimes
Quelquefois

68. Still
Encore

69. Such
Si
(Such and such)
Tel, telle

70. I tell/say
Je dis

71. Thank you
Merci

72. That
Ce, cet, cette

73. The
Le, la, les

74. Their
Leur, leurs

75. Them
Ils, Elles

76. Then
Puis

77. There is
    Il y a

78. They
    Ils

79. Thing
    La chose

80. I think
    Je pense

81. This
    Ce, cet, cette

82. Time
    Temps

83. To
    À

84. Under
    Sous

85. Up here
    Ici
    Up there
    Là-haut

86. Us
    Nous

87. To use
    Utiliser

88. Very
    Très

89. We
    Nous

90. What?
    Comment

91. When
    Quand

92. Where
    Où

93. Which
    Quel

94. Who
    Qui

95. Why
    Pourquoi

96. With
    Avec

97. I would like
    Je voudrais

98. Yes
    Oui

99. You
    Vous, tu

100. Your
    Votre, Vos

© *Use Your Memory*, Tony Buzan, BBC Worldwide Limited.

Past Tense

One of the most useful acronyms for anyone learning French is:

DR. *and* MRS. VAN DER TRAMP

to remember the sixteen verbs that take *être* in the past or perfect tense.

They are:

Verb	Meaning	Past Participle
devenir	to become	devenu
revenir	to come back	revenu
monter	to go up	monté
rester	to stay	resté
sortir	to go out	sorti
venir	to come	venu
aller	to go	allé
naître	to be born	né
descendre	to go down	descendu
entrer	to enter	entré
retourner	to return (somewhere)	retourné
tomber	to fall	tombé
rentrer	to return home	rentré
arriver	to arrive	arrivé
mourir	to die	mort
partir	to leave	parti

ROMANCE LANGUAGES

To recall which are classified as Romance languages, simply think of:

FRIPS

French, Romanian, Italian, Portuguese, Spanish.

GENERAL KNOWLEDGE

"Own only what you can carry with you; know language, know countries, know people. Let your memory be your travel bag."

ALEKSANDR SOLZHENITSYN

This section could as easily have been called "Miscellaneous," or I could have tried to fit each of the topics into more specific sections. However, they seemed to work as a random group of subjects that you may or may not come across or wonder about at some point in everyday life.

BURNING FIREWOOD

My mother-in-law, the most skilled hearth fire maker I know, first made me aware that when it comes to firewood, not all woods are equal. She remembered some but not quite all of this ancient rhyme to guide you in your choice of suitable timber to warm your home:

> Beech log fires burn bright and clear,
> Though only if they're kept a year;
> Store your beech for Christmastide,
> With fresh-cut holly laid beside.
> Chestnut's only good, they say,
> If for years 'tis stored away.
> Birch and fir wood burn too fast,
> Blaze too bright and do not last.

Flames from larch will flicker up high,
Dangerously the sparks will fly.
But ash wood green and ash wood brown
Are fit for a queen with a golden crown.

Oaken logs, if dry and old,
Keep away the winter's cold.
Poplar gives a bitter smoke,
Stings your eyes and makes you choke.
Elm wood burns like churchyard mold,
Even the very flames are cold.
Hawthorn bakes the sweetest bread,
So in Ireland it is said.
Apple wood will scent a room,
Pear wood smells like flowers in bloom.
But ash wood wet and ash wood dry
A king may warm his slippers by.

TEMPERATURES

90 is hot, 70 is nice, 50 is cold, and 30 is ice.

And if you want to know the original version in Celsius, which is definitely more memorable:

30 is hot, 20 is nice, 10 is cold, zero is ice.

CHAMPAGNE BOTTLE SIZES

The smaller ones are easy to remember: there is the usual quarter bottle, half bottle, and bottle. But what comes next?

	Number of standard bottles	
Magnum	2 bottles	1.5 liters
Jeroboam	4 bottles	3 liters
Rehoboam	6 bottles	4.5 liters
Methuselah	8 bottles	6 liters
Salmanazar	12 bottles	9 liters
Balthazar	16 bottles	12 liters
Nebuchadnezzar	20 bottles	15 liters
Melchior	24 bottles	18 liters

The largest of these have a celebratory value but are hardly practical: a Nebuchadnezar weighs almost a staggering eighty-four pounds, and there is some question of quality because pressure can be lost. There are also a few additional sizes occasionally made to mark special occasions or for particular customers. One notable example is the imperial pint-sized bottles that Pol Roger made for Sir Winston Churchill, brought to him promptly each morning at eleven.

All of these bottles are named after biblical, usually Old Testament, figures, with the exception of Magnum, which is alternatively a gun or an '80s TV series starring Tom Selleck.

Jeroboam was the founder and first king of Israel; Rehoboam was the son of King Solomon and ruler of Judah; Methuselah was Noah's grandfather, famed for living to the very grand old age of 969 and dying in the year of the Great Flood; Salmanazar (or Salmaneser) I, II, III, IV, and V were all kings of Assyria; Balthazar was regent of Babylon and also commonly thought to be one of the Three Wise Men; Nebuchadnezzar was the powerful king of Babylon who cast Shadrach, Meshach, and Abednego into the fiery furnace and Daniel into the lion's den (they all miraculously lived to tell the tale); Melchior is another of the Three Wise Men (or Magi) who traveled from the east following the Star of Bethlehem.

This mnemonic may help you remember each bottle in order of size:

M. J. Raps Makes Such Beautiful New Music.

PORT AND STARBOARD

Port and left both have four letters.

Port is traditionally always passed to the left after dinner.

We Left Port and went Right to Starboard.

The terms *port* and *starboard* developed from the earliest days of sailing to avoid any confusion. Starboard is always on the right when facing forward to the front of the boat. The word comes from the Anglo-Saxon *steorbord* for "rudder."

The Old English for the left-hand side was *baecbord*, although from medieval times the word *larboard* was used. This possibly came from *laddebord*, meaning "loading side," because the starboard side with its rudder would always have been kept away from the quay.

The earliest reference to *port* as left is found in Admiral Smyth's *The Sailor's Word Book* of 1867, which states, "The left side of the ship is called port by Admiralty Order, in preference to larboard, as less mistakeable in sound for starboard."

Port Out Starboard Home

The acronym for POSH, or is it? The probably apocryphal explanation is that "port out starboard home" was printed on the more expensive P&O tickets for passengers traveling between Britain and India—the thinking being that as both countries are in the northern hemisphere, port-side cabins were mainly in the shade when traveling out to the east, as were starboard cabins when traveling home to the west. These were the most desirable and therefore expensive cabins, or in other words posh.

Although this is often quoted, it is unlikely. No P&O tickets printed with the phrase have ever been found, although many still exist from the period. Also acronyms are largely twentieth century in origin; few were popular before that, and in fact the word *acronym* wasn't used until the 1940s.

THE LAW

Contracts

OAC

Offer, Acceptance, Consideration.

Torts

"Death Before Dishonor!" Cried Rick.

Duty, Breach of duty, Damage, and Causation that is not too Remote.

BASIC SAFETY

Crossing the Road

In the UK, generations of schoolchildren have been taught the Green Cross Code, which is just a neat way of remembering which way to look before stepping out to safely cross a road. This can be adapted for children in America, where, in common with most of the world apart from the UK, the immediate danger for pedestrians comes from traffic approaching from the left.

Look left, look right, then left again.

First Aid

A first aid lesson for two of us roped in as first aid reps for our floor at one of my first jobs taught me a simple mnemonic for recalling the correct order of response after an accident:

DRAB

Danger, Response, Airways, Breathing.

Danger—assess the situation and any new threats or remaining dangers. For instance, following a car accident, make sure there is a warning for approaching traffic.

Response—check the vital signs of any victims.

Airways—make sure airways are not blocked, by debris or even a victim's own tongue. If victims are semi- or unconscious, it is often best to lay them on their side in the recovery position with the lower arm stretched out and one knee bent.

Breathing—check that victims can breathe by themselves; if not, consider mouth-to-mouth resuscitation.

The word *drab* is also useful for reminding you to behave in a calm manner.

Sports Injuries

For sports injuries, and especially for suspected fractures, sprains, muscle strains, and contusions, remember:

RICE

For 1) Rest, 2) Ice, 3) Compression, 4) Elevation.

And equally important, to know what to avoid, think of:

HARM

For heat, alcohol, running, and massage.

Poison Ivy

Leaves of three, let it be.

I have also heard this with an added line:

Leaves of four, eat some more.

But I wouldn't recommend it without a great deal more information!

Wasp and Bee Stings

I can remember my mother pondering whether it was vinegar for a wasp sting or ammonia as I stood, finger throbbing, feeling sorry for myself. She could never remember which was right and I've always had the same problem. Until I heard a friend chant:

"Use Ammonia for a Bee sting,
And Vinegar for a Wasp sting."

She added, "B follows A and W follows V."

The A to B, V to W is also useful to anyone knowing their Latin family names, because *Apoidae* are Bees while *Vespidae* are Wasps.

Why does this work? Wasp stings are alkaline, so the

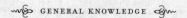

vinegar as an acid neutralizes the poison. Bee stings are acidic, and so ammonia, or more usefully bicarbonate of soda mixed into a paste with water, counters the effects.

Less Basic Safety
Coral and King Snakes

Some king snakes have distinct color bandings very similar to those of coral snakes, making them hard to distinguish. This might not matter except for the fact that while king snakes are harmless, coral snakes are highly venomous—second only to rattlesnakes in potency in North America.

Several rhymes exist to help you tell the difference:

> If red touches black, it's OK Jack,
> If red touches yellow, you're a dead fellow.
>
> Red on yellow, kill a fellow,
> Red on black, don't kill Jack.

And somewhat bluntly:
> If yellow follows red,
> You're dead.

I have to say, I'm sure I'd panic long before getting any one of these right!

OPENING SCREW-TOP JARS AND BOTTLES

It should be so obvious and yet somehow it's so easy to confuse which way to turn a top to open it. This is also useful when wielding a screwdriver:

Righty tighty; lefty loosey.

What could be more simple?

INVESTING

Here are two rhymes giving advice to investors.

Strategy

Don't buy when the market's sky high
And don't sell at the bottom of a well
For you know the market feeds
On people's fear and greed.
The gurus say buy low, sell high,
Easier said than done say I.
Timing the market may lead to profit
But more often is catastrophic.
Forget the fancy computations,
Theoretical models, and speculations:
Look at the trend
And consider it your truest friend,
The surest way to your weight in gold
Is simply to buy and hold.

Interest Rates

When rates are low,
Stocks will grow;
When rates are high,
Stocks will die.

HEREDITARY TITLES

There are five ranks of peer in the United Kingdom, which in descending order are duke, marquess, earl, viscount, and baron.

These can easily be remembered by the sentence:

Don't Make Every Visit Boring.

The title *Lord* is not included because it has various meanings. It is most often used by barons but can be given to the children of dukes and marquesses. It may also be a courtesy title rather than hereditary.

William the Conqueror tried to change the Anglo-Saxon title *Earl* to *Count,* and although he failed, earls' wives are known as countesses. A marchioness is the wife of a marquess, and a baronet is a hereditary title although not a peerage, ranking between a baron and a knight.

The U.S. Constitution specifically prohibits the granting of titles, and some U.S. citizens are not allowed to accept titles of nobility from other countries while they hold office.

Article 1, section 9, clause 8 states:

No title of nobility shall be granted by the United States: and no person holding any office of profit or trust under them, shall, without the consent of the Congress, accept of any present, emolument, office, or title, of any kind whatever, from any king, prince, or foreign state.

THE LOCI, OR JOURNEY, SYSTEM

This is one of the oldest and most widely used mnemonic methods, practiced from classical times and even taught as part of the traditional school curriculum for many years. It is particularly useful for remembering long lists, enabling you to recall many things easily. The great advantage of this method is that you can begin from any point, which distinguishes it from learning by rote, and this explains why it is so popular with actors, speakers, and students studying for exams.

The first record of loci is through an ancient pamphlet called *Rhetorica ad Herennium*, which was written about 85 BC by an unknown Latin author, although the method itself likely predates this period. Cicero refers to loci in *De Oratore*, attributing its invention to Simonides of Ceos. The story goes that he was at a dinner with a number of important Greek nobles and thinkers. Luckily for Simonides, he had just stepped outside when the roof of the building collapsed, crushing the diners below. Simonides was able to identify each of the victims by matching them to their position, or locus, at the table.

The method is basically a peg system that uses locations (loci) with which you are very familiar. Who hasn't dashed upstairs to fetch something, only to forget what it is? The simplest way to remember is to return to your original position, whereupon you can usually recall exactly what you wanted. Loci work in the same way, except the locations you visit to jog your memory are all in the mind.

Picture your home and imagine walking through it. Begin at the front door and move on into the hallway, through the kitchen to the dining room. The more detail you can give to your images, the better, so for instance, concentrate on the ornate hand-shaped knocker on the front door, the distinct terra-cotta and ocher patterned tiles in the hallway, the green glass fruit bowl on the kitchen worktop. Choose specific places in your house and in your mind visit each in turn, always in the same order but visualizing the journey backward as well as forward so that it is fixed firmly in your mind.

The traditional advice is that the mental locations should be well lit, in a definite order and physically fairly evenly spaced and not too far apart. In the sixteenth century, public buildings were usually chosen and the journey was often called a "memory palace"; this helps to give an idea of the sort of mental image you should be creating for yourself.

If you find visualization difficult, think especially of shape and texture when choosing your loci. People who are very musical or who have good auditory memory can use sound as an aid, adding a distinctive soundtrack to their journey.

Once you are familiar with your loci, you can begin to link each point on your journey with items on a list or chunks of a speech represented by distinct objects or symbols. They can then be easily recalled by imagining you are walking through your home, mentally visiting each of your loci. It should become so easy to visualize that you can start your journey at any point, meaning you can remember your list or speech in any order, even backward. The loci can also be used to remember more than one set of items and can be grouped or chunked into small sets as long as they can be mentally visualised in one glance.

As well as choosing detailed, stimulating loci as a starting point, the images you create should also be as vivid as possible. Humorous or incongruous ones are particularly memorable—in 1584 there was furore in England as the Puritans branded the method impious because it encouraged people to think obscene, sacrilegious thoughts. So what are you waiting for? Let your imagination run riot and surprise yourself at just how accurate your memory can be.

As a simple example, picking ten loci in your house, a combination of rooms and furniture, you may have chosen something like the following:

Letter box on the front door
Carpet runner in the hallway
The fridge in your kitchen
The mirror above the fireplace in your sitting room
The sitting room sofa
The stair banister
The sink in your bathroom

The bed in your bedroom
The computer in your study
The bookshelves in the study

And so your mind's journey could be something like this:

The dull brass LETTERBOX with the French word *lettres*
engraved on it is set at hip height on the glossy, scarlet-
painted front door. Walking into the hallway, you step
onto the striped terra-cotta and straw-colored CARPET
RUNNER and walk to the kitchen, where you see the
baby-blue, chubby FRIDGE standing in the
corner. Turning, you make your way to the sitting room,
where you glance at your reflection in the slightly hazed
MIRROR with the ornate frame that hangs above the
fireplace. Next, you slump comfortably onto the purple
velvet SOFA. Climbing the stairs, you run your hands
over the smooth, polished wooden BANISTER. In the
bathroom you wash your hands in the SINK with the
nickel taps. You walk along the landing to your bedroom
and look at your metal-framed BED with its white duvet
and patterned quilt. Work in mind, you return along the
landing to your small study with the white laptop COM-
PUTER on your desk and the tall overstocked BOOK-
SHELVES next to the window.

Once your journey is fixed in your mind with each detailed locus in order, you can use it to memorize anything you want, from facts for exams, to speeches or lists of information. With practice, this can become an incredibly flexible memory system, its potential limited only by how creative you can be.

Begin simply with an easy list:

Basket
Towel
Shampoo
Pineapple
DVD
Deodorant
Cell phone
Newspaper
Pens
Bar of chocolate

The idea is to associate each item on the list with a stage of your journey, making it as vivid and memorable as possible. For example:

A wicker shopping basket has been wedged into the large brass letterbox. You struggle to free it, tugging hard until it suddenly shoots into the hallway, spilling the bright orange towel that was inside out onto the striped carpet runner. You walk into the kitchen, where an open bottle of shampoo is lying on its side on top of the fridge, creamy shampoo slowly oozing down the pale blue surface. In the sitting room a large pineapple on the fireplace is reflected in the mirror, moldering in the heat from the fire. You sit down on the squidgy purple sofa, suddenly uncomfortable as a DVD splinters as you sit on it. Walking upstairs, the normally smooth banister is sticky with sickly smelling deodorant. You go to wash your hands in the bathroom sink, only to find it blocked by a giant cell phone. Walking to your bedroom, you are surprised to find your bed covered by newspaper instead of the usual white duvet and quilt. In the study your white laptop is scrawled with squiggled pen marks, the pens lying next to it in pools of colored ink. You look up to see that the bookshelves are stocked with giant bars of chocolate in place of books.

You will find that as you mentally walk through your journey visiting each locus, you will clearly see each item on your list. And what's more, you will still remember them even after a gap of some time.

MEMORY PALACES

With a view to expanding the possibilities for memory offered by the Loci System, you can take the technique to a higher level by adding to your journeys and rooms. You can begin by expanding them within your home—for instance, mentally stepping inside your wardrobe, the understairs cupboard, or even the contents of your fridge. But it can also help to create or add new rooms.

Some experts suggest creating imaginary locations, but I think this takes quite some time to really fix in your mind, and the temptation is to change or improve details, which all gets very confusing. Instead, I would recommend choosing somewhere you already know well, preferably somewhere you like that you can mentally access from a door or via a corridor you add to your original loci. Your childhood home, a favorite well-visited museum or gallery, a friend's home, or even somewhere you holiday can all work well, just as long as you can picture it vividly and there are plenty of interesting details to use as hooks. If you visit somewhere that appeals, photograph it to permanently fix the minutiae ready to be used later.

At this point you might also find it helpful to add markers every so often. The ancient Greeks suggested a marker every five loci so that you can easily pick up at any point. The fifth one could be marked by a star with five points, number twelve by a dozen eggs: whatever appeals to you. Classical scholars also thought it important that the loci on your journey be well spaced: they recommended they should be at least two yards apart. I don't really think this is necessary just as long as they are distinct.

The addition of extra rooms, creating a vast memory palace, allows you to keep some rooms as permanent stores for information, poetry, and facts you know you want to remember forever. Your can shut and open the door on them at will and keep them quite separate from anything else you may have stored.

HISTORY

"To be ignorant of what happened before you were born is to be ever a child. For what is man's lifetime unless the memory of past events is woven with those of earlier times?"

MARCUS TULLIUS CICERO

Once I started thinking about history in general, I surprised myself by how many different mnemonics I remembered, at least in part, most of which I learned at school. Historical facts and stories have been the inspiration for many poems and songs, including Christopher Columbus's voyage of discovery in 1492 and Paul Revere's midnight ride. It was often "baddies" who inspired the most lively and inventive mnemonics, presumably because their stories are more colorful—just think of the Tudor king Henry VIII and his six unfortunate wives. I also discovered a satisfyingly precise one for the exact date, including the hour, at which prohibition was lifted in Finland—read on to find out more.

PERIODS OF HISTORY

Pupils Eat Grapes Regularly During Morning Registration In Toilets.

Should help with:

Prehistoric, Egyptian, Greek, Roman, Dark Ages, Medieval, Renaissance, Industrial Revolution, Twentieth Century and beyond.

THE SEVEN WONDERS OF THE ANCIENT WORLD

Ebenezer Cobham Brewer (1810–1897) is probably best remembered as the author of *Brewer's Dictionary of Phrase and Fable,* which is still in print. He wrote a verse listing the Seven Wonders, though, rather confusingly, uses Roman rather than Greek names for goddesses:

> *The Pyramids first, which in Egypt were laid;*
> *Then Babylon's Gardens, for Amytis made;*
> *Third, Mausolus' Tomb, of affection and guilt;*
> *Fourth, the Temple of Dian, in Ephesus built;*
> *Fifth, Colossus of Rhodes, cast in bronze, to the sun;*
> *Sixth, Jupiter's Statue, by Philidas done;*
> *The Pharos of Egypt, last wonder of old,*
> *Or the Palace of Cyrus, cemented with gold.*

That is:

1. The Great Pyramid of Giza.
2. The Hanging Gardens of Babylon in Baghdad.
3. The Tomb of Mausolus at Halicarnassus in Greece
4. The Temple of Diana (or Artemis) at Ephesus.
5. The Colossus of Rhodes.
6. The Statue of Jupiter (or Zeus, which was the Greek name) at Olympia.
7. The Pharos, or Lighthouse, at Alexandria.

The ancient Greeks loved making lists, and the Palace of Cyrus is occasionally included as a wonder. According to

Herodotus it was built at Ecbatana, in Persia, on the orders of Deioces.

The earliest lists claim the Ishtar Gate as the seventh wonder. This was the eighth gate to the inner city of Babylon, built by order of King Nebuchadnezzar II, dedicated to the goddess Ishtar. The gate was replaced by the Lighthouse of Alexandria in the sixth century.

EGYPTIAN PHAROAHS

The New Kingdom covered the eighteenth, nineteenth, and twentieth dynasties of ancient Egypt from the sixteenth to the eleventh century BC. The period saw the Egyptian empire at its greatest territorially, stretching from Nubia in the south through the Near East, with Egyptian armies fighting the Hittites for control of Syria.

The pharaohs of the first two dynasties of the Egyptian New Kingdom are:

Ahmose I, Amenhotep I, Thutmose I, Thutmose II, Thutmose III, Hatshepsut, Amenhotep II, Thutmose IV, Amenhotep III (the Magnificent king), Akhenaten, Smenhakare, Tutankhamun, Ay, Horemheb (eighteenth dynasty).

Ramesses I, Seti I, Ramesses II (the Great, also the ruler associated with Moses), Merneptah, Amenemses, Seti II, Merneptah, Siptah, Tausret (nineteenth dynasty).

Here is a slightly convoluted mnemonic sentence for them:

An Apple That Thinks Thinks Heavily And Thinks All Apples Sometimes Think Apparently Has Really Serious Ramifications Mentally And Saves More Serious Thought.

The ten pharaohs of the twentieth dynasty are simpler to learn because you only have to remember two names:

Setnakhte, Rameses III, IV, V, VI, VII, VIII, IX, X, XI.

DISCOVERY OF THE NEW WORLD

Columbus set sail at dawn on August 2, 1492, in search of the East Indies, testing the relatively new theory that the world was round. He sailed under the Spanish flag with three ships, the *Niña*, the *Pinta*, and the flagship, the *Santa María*. The theory was of course correct, but Columbus greatly underestimated the circumference of the world and had not expected to come across the American continent. He finally landed on October 12, 1492, in the Bahamas. He went on to make three further voyages of discovery, the final one in 1502, and established settlements and trade routes.

Most people remember the date of the first voyage from the children's poem:

> In fourteen hundred and ninety-two
> Columbus sailed the ocean blue.
> He had three ships and left from Spain;
> He sailed through sunshine, wind, and rain.

He sailed by night; he sailed by day;
He used the stars to find his way.
A compass also helped him know
How to find the way to go.

Ninety sailors were on board;
Some men worked while others snored.
Then the workers went to sleep;
And others watched the ocean deep.

Day after day they looked for land;
They dreamed of trees and rocks and sand.
October 12th their dream came true,
You never saw a happier crew!

"Indians! Indians!" Columbus cried;
His heart was filled with joyful pride.
But "India" the land was not;
It was the Bahamas, and it was hot.

The Arakawa natives were very nice;
They gave the sailors food and spice.
Columbus sailed on to find some gold
To bring back home, as he'd been told.

He made the trip again and again,
Trading gold to bring to Spain.
The first American? No, not quite.
But Columbus was brave, and he was bright.

We now know that Columbus was not the first European to discover the Americas: Viking sailors almost certainly landed there, and archaeological evidence suggests that Leif Eriksson, an eleventh-century Icelandic explorer, was actually the first to arrive, founding a settlement in Newfoundland. However, it was Columbus who really began the process of European colonization.

Columbus Day was first celebrated unofficially from the latter part of the eighteenth century and was fixed as the second Monday in October in 1971, although there has since been a trend away from commemorating the day.

THIRTEEN STATES FROM
THIRTEEN COLONIES

Virginia, in 1607, was the first of the thirteen colonies to be founded, and Georgia was the last, in 1733. They were part of what was known as British America until the Treaty of Paris recognized their independence in 1783.

This is a useful mnemonic for remembering them:

Cory Doesn't Give My Mom's Nutty New Noisy Neighbor Pam Rides in Susie's Van.

Connecticut, Delaware, Georgia, Maryland, Massachusetts, New Hampshire, New Jersey, New York, North Carolina, Pennsylvania, Rhode Island, South Carolina, Virginia.

Or you may prefer:

My Nifty New Car Needs Re Painting. Maybe Deep Violet? No Shiny Gold!

Although these thirteen colonies can be considered members of the United States from the Declaration of Independence on July 4, 1776, the order in which they became states depends on the date each ratified the Constitution:

1. Delaware, December 7, 1787
2. Pennsylvania, December 12, 1787
3. New Jersey, December 18, 1787
4. Georgia, January 2, 1788
5. Connecticut, January 9, 1788
6. Massachusetts, February 6, 1788
7. Maryland, April 28, 1788
8. South Carolina, May 23, 1788
9. New Hampshire, June 21, 1788
10. Virginia, June 25, 1788
11. New York, July 26, 1788
12. North Carolina, November 21, 1789
13. Rhode Island, May 29, 1790

Delia Picked Nice Juicy Grapes'n Cherries Making Mary Some Clearly Natural Vitamin Nourishing Neo-Colonial Risotto.

THE AMERICAN REVOLUTION

The American Revolution, also known as the American War of Independence in European countries, began with the rebellion of the thirteen original colonies against British rule in 1775. They first rejected British government and later the British monarchy. The colonies united to form a provisional government, formally proclaiming independence as a new nation on July 4, 1776.

Other European nations soon joined the conflict. The French, Spanish, and Dutch fought against the British, who were supported by Germany. The war finally came to an end in 1783, when the Treaty of Paris officially recognized the sovereignty of the United States over territory bounded by Canada to the north, the Mississippi River to the west, and Florida to the south.

Paul Revere

Paul Revere was baptized on January 1, 1735, and he died May 10, 1818. He was a silversmith and American patriot, celebrated after his death for his role as messenger in the battles of Lexington and Concord in the American Revolutionary War.

His famed "Midnight Ride" took place on the night of April 18–19, 1775, when he and William Dawes were asked to ride from Boston to Lexington to warn John Hancock and Samuel Adams of the movement of the British army, who were planning to seize the weapons store in Concord and at the same time arrest Hancock and Adams. The poem was written by the American poet Henry Wadsworth Longfellow in 1860 and tells a fictionalized account of Revere as narrated by the landlord of the Wayside Inn.

> Now listen my children and you shall hear
> Of the midnight ride of Paul Revere,
> On the eighteenth of April, in Seventy-five;
> Hardly a man is now alive
> Who remembers that famous day and year.

The poem goes on to relate the heroic events of the night, but in fact Revere and Dawes were joined by Dr. Samuel Prescott on the road and were then stopped by British troops at Lincoln. Dawes and Prescott escaped, while Revere was escorted at gunpoint back to Lexington. Of the three, only Prescott actually arrived in Concord in time to warn the American militia.

And if you are concerned to remember William Dawes, who initially set out with Revere, you might like Helen F. Moore's parody of Longfellow, written in 1896:

> 'Tis all very well for the children to hear
> Of the midnight ride of Paul Revere;
> But why should my name be quite forgot,
> Who rode as boldly and well, God wot?
> Why should I ask? The reason is clear—
> My name was Dawes and his Revere.

Did You Know?

On July 4, 1826, the fiftieth anniversary of the founding of the United States, both the second (John Adams) and third (Thomas Jefferson) presidents died within a few hours of each other.

The American Constitution

In 1787 the Founding Fathers set out the principles of the Constitution. The first part is called the Preamble, and many schoolchildren, when asked to learn it, have found that the *Schoolhouse Rock* song is the easiest way to remember it. The first line in the song is altered, leaving out "of the United States," but the rest is correct. The real Preamble reads:

> *We the people of the United States, in order to form a more perfect union, establish justice, insure domestic tranquility, provide for the common defense, promote the general welfare, and secure the blessings of liberty to ourselves and our posterity, do ordain and establish this Constitution for the United States of America.*

The Constitution sets out the fundamental principles and purposes of the United States. It was accepted by the Constitutional Convention on September 17, 1787, in Philadelphia, Pennsylvania, and formally ratified by conventions in each state. The original document was handwritten by Jacob Shallus, and you can see it displayed in the National Archives and Records Administration in Washington, D.C.

The Constitution has been amended twenty-seven times to date. The first ten amendments are known as the Bill of Rights.

Easily memorable are:

- The amendment restricting a president to two terms of office is 22.
- The Prohibition amendments are conveniently numbers 18 and 21.

Did You Know?

The U.S. Constitution is not only the oldest but also the shortest national constitution still in use today.

The Founding Fathers

Historians used to view the Founding Fathers as the "Signers," those who signed the Declaration of Independence, and the "Framers," who helped draft the Constitution. Now the term generally applies to a wider group, including all those who were involved in winning independence and creating the United States. These seven are most often cited:

George Washington, John Adams, Thomas Jefferson, Benjamin Franklin, Alexander Hamilton, James Madison, and John Jay.

Remember them by:

Will Adam Join Frank Helping Make Jam.

WAR OF 1812

The 1812 war between the United States and Britain was primarily over trade restrictions, but it was also about objections to the forced recruitment of U.S. citizens into the Royal Navy and British support for Native Americans. It was fought mainly along the Atlantic coastline, the U.S.–Canadian frontier, and the coast of the Gulf of Mexico. It ended with the Treaty of Ghent, signed by the British in December 1814 and ratified by the United States on February 16, 1815.

In Britain the war was largely overshadowed by the Napoleonic wars in Europe, but several battles in particular captured the imagination of the American public, reflected in songs and poems of the time. Most notably, the Defense of Baltimore inspired the lyrics of the National Anthem, "The Star-Spangled Banner."

The Defense of Baltimore and
"The Star-Spangled Banner"

The Defense of Baltimore, or the Battle of Fort McHenry, in 1813, was not really a battle at all, as the British ship bombarding the fort in Chesapeake Bay was out of range of U.S. guns, but it was dramatic enough for Francis Scott Key, a lawyer and amateur poet, to write "The Defense of Fort McHenry."

The poem was set to the tune of a popular British drinking song, written by John Stafford Smith for one of the gentlemen's clubs in London, and it eventually became "The Star-pangled Banner." The song was adopted as the National

Anthem by a congressional resolution in 1931, signed by President Hoover. Previously, "Hail Columbia" was usually sung at official functions.

The Star-Spangled Banner

O! say can you see by the dawn's early light
What so proudly we hailed at the twilight's last gleaming?
Whose broad stripes and bright stars through the perilous
    fight,
O'er the ramparts we watched were so gallantly streaming?
And the rockets' red glare, the bombs bursting in air,
Gave proof through the night that our flag was still there.
O! say does that star-spangled banner yet wave
O'er the land of the free and the home of the brave?

On the shore, dimly seen through the mists of the deep,
Where the foe's haughty host in dread silence reposes,
What is that which the breeze, o'er the towering steep,
As it fitfully blows, half conceals, half discloses?
Now it catches the gleam of the morning's first beam,
In full glory reflected now shines in the stream:
'Tis the star-spangled banner! Oh long may it wave
O'er the land of the free and the home of the brave.

And where is that band who so vauntingly swore
That the havoc of war and the battle's confusion,
A home and a country should leave us no more!
Their blood has washed out their foul footsteps' pollution.

No refuge could save the hireling and slave
From the terror of flight, or the gloom of the grave:
And the star-spangled banner in triumph doth wave
O'er the land of the free and the home of the brave.

O! thus be it ever, when freemen shall stand
Between their loved home and the war's desolation!
Blest with victory and peace, may the heav'n rescued land
Praise the Power that hath made and preserved us a nation.
Then conquer we must, when our cause it is just,
And this be our motto: "In God is our trust."
And the star-spangled banner in triumph shall wave
O'er the land of the free and the home of the brave!

The Stars and Stripes Flag

Also affectionately nicknamed "Old Glory" and "The Star-Spangled Banner," the original thirteen-star version of the flag was adopted on June 14, 1777. The thirteen stars represented the thirteen colonies and, later, the states of the United States. As more states joined the union, stars were added to the flag, until the fifty-star version became official on July 4, 1960, after Hawaii and then Alaska gained statehood.

It was settled in 1916 that there should be more red than white stripes, and President Eisenhower declared in 1959 that earlier versions of the flag could still be used as long as they were in good order.

The American flag is a strong symbol of the country and can also be viewed as a useful reminder: there are fifty stars for each of the fifty states and thirteen equal horizontal stripes representing the thirteen original colonies.

The Battle of New Orleans

The final battle of the 1812 war began on December 23, 1814, and the invading British army was finally defeated by Andrew Jackson on January 8, 1815. It was immortalized in a song by a musical high school principal named Jimmy Driftwood. He understood just how useful songs could be and loved writing them to help his students learn. His song "The Battle of New Orleans" was so popular it won the 1959 Grammy Award for best country and western performance.

Even without the music it's easy to memorize. It begins:

> Well in eighteen and fourteen we took a little trip
> Along with Colonel Jackson down the mighty Mississip.
> We took a little bacon and we took a little beans,
> And we caught the bloody British near the town of New
>   Orleans.

AMERICAN CIVIL WAR

The Civil War broke out in 1861 after John Brown raided Harpers Ferry. Eleven southern states seceded from the union to declare themselves the Confederate States of America. During the course of the next four years there were more than ten thousand military actions, many relatively small skirmishes rather than big battles. The loss of life was devastating for both soldiers and civilians, and the country was permanently scarred. With notable defeats for the Confederates at Gettysburg and Vicksburg, Robert E. Lee finally surrendered to Ulysses S. Grant, general in chief of the Union army, at Appomattox Court House on April 9, 1865, and the authority of the federal government was restored.

Secession of the Confederate States

To recall the order of secession of the Confederate States of America after the Civil War, think of:

So My Father Ate Grapes Last Tuesday, Very Awesome Tart Napas.

South Carolina, Mississippi, Florida, Alabama, Georgia, Louisiana, Texas.

The comma after "Tuesday" represents Lincoln's call for troops, after which four further states seceded: Virginia, Arkansas, Tennessee, North Carolina.

There is actually some controversy over which state was the last to secede, Tennessee or North Carolina.

Five Years of War

The key events of the Civil War can be recalled chronologically:

In 1861 the war began   (War technically begins)
In 1862 the bullets flew   (First battles are fought)

In 1863 Lincoln set the slaves free	(Final draft of President Lincoln's Emancipation Proclamation)
In 1864 there was still a war	
In 1865 hardly a man is left alive	(War finally ends, but with great loss of life)

U.S. PRESIDENTS

To remember the first presidents, just ask yourself:

Will A Jolly Man Make A Just But Harshly Treated President?

Washington, Adams, Jefferson, Madison, Monroe, (Quincy) Adams, Jackson, Van Buren, Harrison, Tyler, Polk.

The middle U.S. presidents can be recalled:

Taylor Felt Proud But Lincoln Just Grinned, Happily Gargling, And Could Hardly Contain McKinley.

Taylor, Fillmore, Pierce, Buchanan, Lincoln, Johnson, Grant, Hayes, Garfield, Arthur, Cleveland, Harrison, Cleveland, McKinley.

Or if you prefer, this is probably easier to remember for the first fourteen presidents:

When A Joke Made Me A Joker, Van Had To Poke The Fiery Poker.

Washington, Adams, Jefferson, Madison, Monroe, (Quincy) Adams, Jackson, Van Buren, Harrison, Tyler, Polk, Taylor, Fillmore, Pierce.

The presidents of the twentieth century, using several of their names:

Theodore Takes Wilson's Hand Coolly Hoovering Franklin's True Experiences. Ken, Justly Noted For Candor, Rules But Calmly.

Theodore Roosevelt, Taft, Wilson, Harding, Coolidge, Hoover, Franklin D. Roosevelt, Truman, Eisenhower, Kennedy, Johnson, Nixon, Ford, Carter, Reagan, Bush, Clinton.

The complete list with the dates of their presidencies is:

1. George Washington,1789–1797
2. John Adams, 1797–1801
3. Thomas Jefferson, 1801–1809
4. James Madison, 1809–1817
5. James Monroe, 1817–1825
6. John Quincy Adams, 1825–1829 (He was the first president who was also the son of a president.)
7. Andrew Jackson, 1829–1837
8. Martin Van Buren, 1837–1841
9. William Henry Harrison, 1841 (In office less than a month, he caught a cold and died of pneumonia on April 4, the first president to die in office.)
10. John Tyler, 1841–1845 (Dubbed "his Accidency," he was the first vice president to become president following the death of his predecessor.)
11. James K. Polk, 1845–1849
12. Zachary Taylor, 1849–1850 (He fell ill and died after Fourth of July ceremonies.)

13. Millard Fillmore, 1850–1853
14. Franklin Pierce, 1853–1857
15. James Buchanan, 1857–1861
16. Abraham Lincoln, 1861–1865 (On Good Friday, April 14, 1865, Lincoln was assassinated by the actor John Wilkes Booth, who mistakenly thought his action would help the South.)
17. Andrew Johnson, 1865–1869
18. Ulysses S. Grant, 1869–1877
19. Rutherford B. Hayes, 1877–1881
20. James Garfield, 1881 (On July 2, 1881, Garfield was shot by an embittered attorney. He lay wounded for weeks, dying on September 19.)
21. Chester Alan Arthur, 1881–1885
22. Grover Cleveland, 1885–1889 (He was the first Democrat to be elected after the Civil War, and the only president to leave office and return for a second term four years later.)
23. Benjamin Harrison, 1889–1893
24. Grover Cleveland, 1893–1897
25. William McKinley, 1897–1901 (His second term as president came to a sad end when he was shot by an anarchist in September 1901.)
26. Theodore Roosevelt, 1901–1909 (At forty-three he became the youngest president until that time.)
27. William H. Taft, 1909–1913
28. Woodrow Wilson, 1913–1921 (He took the United States into the First World War in 1917.)

29. Warren G. Harding, 1921–1923
30. Calvin Coolidge, 1923–1929
31. Herbert Hoover, 1929–1933
32. Franklin D. Roosevelt, 1933–1945
33. Harry S. Truman, 1945–1953
34. Dwight D. Eisenhower, 1953–1961
35. John Fitzgerald Kennedy, 1961–1963 (He was the youngest man to be elected president and the youngest to die in office. He had just passed one thousand days in office when he was assassinated in Dallas, Texas.)
36. Lyndon B. Johnson, 1963–1969
37. Richard M. Nixon, 1969–1974 (He was infamous for the Watergate scandal.)
38. Gerald Ford, 1974–1977
39. Jimmy Carter, 1977–1981
40. Ronald Reagan, 1981–1989
41. George H. W. Bush, 1989–1993
42. William (Bill) Jefferson Clinton, 1993–2001
43. George W. Bush, 2001–2009
44. Barack H. Obama, 2009–

The Presidential Heads Carved on Mount Rushmore

We Just Like Rushmore.

George Washington, Thomas Jefferson, Abraham Lincoln, Theodore Roosevelt.

Mount Rushmore National Memorial, near Keystone, South Dakota, was carved by the sculptor Gutzon Borglum. It represents the first 150 years of U.S. history, with sixty-foot-high sculptures of the four presidents.

PROHIBITION

Prohibition refers to a law banning the manufacture, sale, and transportation, including importing and exporting, of alcohol to drink. The term is usually taken to refer to the laws passed during the first half of the twentieth century as a result of pressure from the Protestant temperance movement, which warned against the evils of alcohol.

It was most famously enforced in the United States from October 28, 1919, until the Great Depression, when President Franklin D. Roosevelt amended the law on March 23, 1933, to allow the manufacture and sale of certain types of alcoholic drink. The law was finally repealed on December 5 of that year. However, the United States was not the only country to pass laws of prohibition, as the temperance movement was also particularly strong in Scandinavia:

1900–1948, Prince Edward Island and other parts of Canada for shorter periods
1914–1925, Russia and the USSR
1915–1922, Iceland (beer remained banned until 1989)
1916–1927, Norway
1919, Hungary
1919–1932, Finland

There is a rather neat, though probably not very useful, mnemonic for the exact moment that prohibition was lifted in Finland:

543210

The 5th of the 4th month in 1932 at 10 in the morning.

FIRST FLIGHT

In nineteen hundred and three, the Wright brothers flew free.

This recalls the world's first successful "sustained and controlled" powered flight. It took place on December 17, 1903, by the pioneering brothers Wilbur and Orville Wright, in the Wright Flyer I, from Kill Devil Hills, North Carolina. The plane can now be seen in the Smithsonian Institution in Washington, D.C.

THE DARK AGES

Knights of the Round Table

I realize that strictly speaking this is not history, but as an enduring element of Dark Ages mythology, it seems worth including King Arthur's famous Knights of the Round Table.

There are many versions of the legend and different authors disagree about how many knights there actually were, but these ten are generally accepted by most:

Lancelot, Galahad, Mark, Mordred, Tristram, Gawain,
Palomides, Kay, Tor, Lamorack.

They can be called to mind by:

Lance Gallantly Made Muffins To Give Paul's Kite The Lead.

ENGLISH KINGS AND QUEENS

As with many mnemonics, the origin of the rhyme is not
known but it is at least a hundred years old, with additions to
cover the extra monarchs.

Willie, Willie, Harry, Steve,
Harry, Dick, John, Harry Three,
One Two Three Neds, Richard Two,
Harrys Four Five Six . . . then who?
Edwards Four Five, Dick the Bad,
Harrys twain, Ned Six the lad,
Mary, Bessie, James you ken,
Then Charlie, Charlie, James again . . .
Will and Mary, Anne of Gloria,
Georges (four), Will Four, Victoria,
Edward Seven next, and then came George the Fifth in
*   1910 . . .*
Ned the Eighth soon abdicated,
So George the Sixth was coronated,
Then number Two Elizabeth . . .
And that's all folks (until her death . . .).

A shortened version for the last few lines following on from Victoria is:

> *Edward Seven, Georgie Five,*
> *Edward, George and Liz (alive).*

Written in full the order of rulers is:

> William the Conqueror (I), William II Rufus, Henry I,
> Stephen, Henry II, Richard I (the Lionheart), John,
> Henry III, Edward I (Longshanks), Edward II, Edward III,
> Richard II, Henry IV, Henry V, Henry VI, Edward IV,
> Edward V, Richard III, Henry VII, Henry VIII, Edward VI,
> Mary I, Elizabeth I, James I (and VI of Scotland), Charles I,
> Charles II, James II, William and Mary II, Anne, George I,
> George II, George III, George IV, William IV, Victoria,
> Edward VII, George V, Edward VIII, George VI,
> Elizabeth II.

This sentence can help with the first fourteen:

> *Working Wives Have Seldom Had Racily Jazzy Hemlines,*
> *Triple E Rubber Hardly Helps.*

William the Conqueror

There is also:

> *William the First was the first of our kings,*
> *Not counting Ethelreds, Egberts, and things . . .*

> ### *King John*
> And to bring to mind one of our worst monarchs:
>
> *Bad, bad, bad King John,*
> *Shamed the throne that he sat upon.*
> *Not a scruple, not a straw, cared this monarch for the law.*

ROYAL DYNASTIES

No Plan Like Yours To Study History Suitably Well.

Norman (1066–1154), Plantagenet (1154–1399),
Lancastrian (from 1399), York (from 1461),
Tudor (1485–1603), Stuart (1603–1649, 1660–1714),
Hanoverian (1714–1901), Saxe-Coburg and Gotha
(1901–1917, when the dynasty was renamed), Windsor
(from 1917 until the present day).

This is a rather simplified version, omitting houses that
did not actually become dynasties, namely: Blois 1135–54;
Angevin 1154–1216, which effectively became the Plan-
tagenets; and Orange 1689–1702, when William of Orange
ruled jointly with Queen Mary Stuart. The dynasty changes
back and forth between Lancaster and York during the Wars of
the Roses are not reflected, simply the earliest date for the rule
of both. It also makes no mention of the Commonwealth—
including the Protectorate of Oliver Cromwell (1653–1658,

following the beheading of King Charles I in 1649)—which lasted until 1660, when the monarchy was reinstated under King Charles II.

GOLDEN JUBILEE MONARCHS

A golden jubilee celebrates fifty years of a monarch's reign, and the present Queen Elizabeth marked hers in 2002 with a tour of the UK and Commonwealth, concerts, a service of thanksgiving, and a procession along The Mall. Although the idea of an actual ceremony to celebrate seems to have begun with Queen Victoria in 1887, three earlier British monarchs also reached this landmark.

Henry III 1216–1272 (56 years)·
Edward III 1327–1377 (50 years)
George III 1760–1820 (59 years)

As each king is a "third," this line is a helpful reminder:

Vicky victorious and three of the Thirds,
And now there is also Elizabeth Two.

James I reigned in England for twenty-two years, from 1603 until 1625, but was actually King James VI of Scotland for fifty-seven years, 1567–1625.

The Six Wives of Henry VIII

Henry VIII ruled from 1509 until 1547. He was a Renaissance man, his court being a center for scholarly learning, art, and music. Among many notable events, including the struggle with Rome and ultimately the separation of the Anglican Church, dissolution of the monasteries, and establishment of the monarch as the supreme head of the Church of England, Henry is infamous for marrying six wives:

Catherine of Aragon (1485–1536) married 1510. The widow of Henry's older brother Arthur and the mother of Mary I.

Anne Boleyn (1507–1536) married 1533. Anne was maid of honor to Catherine of Aragon and the mother of Elizabeth I.

Jane Seymour (1509–1537) married 1536. Jane was lady-in-waiting to both Catherine and Anne. She died of a fever following the birth of Edward VI. She is buried beside Henry VIII at Windsor Castle.

Anne of Cleves (1515–1557) married 1540. She was the daughter of the Duke of Cleves, in Germany. The marriage was never consummated, and after the annulment she was given a generous settlement. Anne outlived all Henry's other wives.

Catherine Howard (1522–1542) married 1540. She was just twenty-two when Henry had her beheaded for treason after she was found guilty of adultery.

Catherine Parr (1512–1548) married 1542. Henry was actually her third husband, and she went on to marry for a fourth time, dying of what at the time was called childbed fever, the same illness that claimed the life of Jane Seymour.

There are several well-known rhymes about his wives:

Kate an' Anne an' Jane,
an' Anne an' Kate again, again.

This recalls their names in order of succession. The second has helped decades of school children remember the usually unfortunate fate of each:

Divorced, beheaded, died.
Divorced, beheaded, survived.

And finally:

Prince Hal of York to six wives was wedded,
One died, one survived, two divorced, and two beheaded.

Or to prompt their surnames:

Arrogant	Bull	Sees	Cleaner's	Hair	Parted
Aragon	Boleyn	Seymour	Cleves	Howard	Parr

And their children:

Mary Elizabeth Edward None None None

Henry's reputation for dispensing with his chancellors was not much better than with his wives. Just remember that all four were called Thomas and that they conveniently follow in reverse alphabetical order:

Thomas Wolsey
Died on the way to trial
Built Hampton Court

Sir Thomas More
Executed

Thomas Cromwell
Executed

Thomas Cranmer
Survived—though later
burned at the stake by Mary I

CAUSES OF THE FIRST WORLD WAR

Just ask yourself, what are the four MAIN causes of World War I?
Answer: Militarism, Alliance, Imperialism, Nationalism.

KEY DATES

1066 and All That

The Battle of Hastings in 1066
When William the Conqueror started his tricks.

The Hundred Years War

Lasting from 1336 until 1453, the war actually lasted 117 years.
Interestingly, the number of letters and spaces in Hundred
Years War adds up to 17, so just add 17 to 100.

It was begun by Edward III in a bid for complete sovereignty
over the duchy of Aquitaine in southwest France. The war
escalated under Henry V into an attempt to conquer the whole
of France, leading to such memorable battles as Agincourt on
St. Crispin's Day, October 25, 1415, and the appearance of Joan
of Arc as France's savior at the Siege of Orléans in 1429 (she
was burned at the stake at Rouen in 1431 at the age of nineteen
and finally canonized in 1920).

The Fire of London

The Fire began in Thomas Farynor's bakery in Pudding Lane,
close to London Bridge, shortly after midnight on Sunday,
September 2, 1666. It blazed on through great swaths of the
city until it was finally quenched on Wednesday, September 5.
Much of the medieval City of London within the old Roman
walls was destroyed, although the West End, Westminster, and
Charles II's palace at Whitehall escaped the flames.

It is possible that more of the city could have been saved if
the widescale demolitions suggested by firefighters had been
carried out sooner. The lord mayor, Sir Thomas Bloodworth,
was blamed for the delay, famously remarking about the blaze,
"Pish! A woman could piss it out." Samuel Pepys wrote in
detail about the events in his diary, commenting, "It made me
weep to see it."

Despite many radical plans for rebuilding, the city was
largely reconstructed on the original street plan that existed
before the fire.

The year 1666 can be represented by a simple diagram
showing the 6s as chimneys with smoke rising.

Or, I think, easier to bring to mind is:

In sixteen hundred and sixty-six,
London burned like rotten sticks.

Nelson and Napoleon

Vice Admiral Horatio Nelson defeated Napoleon on October 21, 1805, at the Battle of Trafalgar, during which he was killed. He was also injured during several earlier battles, losing both his right eye (the 1794 capture of Corsica) and right arm (in the 1797 Battle of Santa Cruz). The order in which he sustained his injuries can be remembered simply by the word:

EARS

Eye, Arm—both Rights

After the Battle of Trafalgar, Napoleon was defeated at the Battle of Toulouse in 1814, after which he was exiled to the island of Elba. A well-known palindrome records this:

Able was I ere I saw Elba.

Napoleon actually escaped from Elba and was finally defeated by Wellington at the Battle of Waterloo in 1815, after which he was exiled to the far Atlantic island of St. Helena, where he died in 1821.

THE PEG AND MAJOR SYSTEMS—THE NUMBER/RHYME MNEMONIC

The Peg System uses numbers instead of words and is particularly useful for learning anything involving figures—telephone numbers, bank accounts, PIN codes, dates, or any of the other numbers we can struggle to remember correctly every day.

To work the system you must memorize a list of words that are easy to associate with the numbers they represent. Generally the list has to be memorized only once, after which it can be used many times. It is usually easiest to remember the words if they rhyme. So your list could go something like this:

One	Gun
Two	Shoe
Three	Tree
Four	Door
Five	Hive
Six	Sticks
Seven	Heaven
Eight	Gate
Nine	Wine
Ten	Pen

Although this is very easy to remember, it is limited in the number of pegs it can produce. Rhyming is also more difficult once you reach the teens and above. You can over-come this by repeating the same images in each group of ten, so for instance 15, 25, 35, 45, 55, etc., can all be hives with bees, but each group of ten can be represented differ-ently, so 11–20 could be hot and sunny, 21–30 snowy cold, 31–40 red, 41–50 green, and so on. However, this could quickly become very complex.

The Major System develops the Peg System further, making it possible to remember much longer numbers. It works by converting each number into a consonant sound and then into words by adding vowels. The words are more easily remembered than the numbers, especially if you make sure the words themselves are memorable as you would with any other memory system.

Digits from 0 to 9 are represented by different con-sonants, the choice of letters dictated by those we most readily connect with each number. Vowels and the letters w, h, and y are not assigned to a particular digit and can be used as fillers to make up useful words. The choice of consonants varies and you can draw up your own, but the most popular list is:

Digit	Letters	Explanation
0	s/z	Z is the first letter of zero, and s is the most similar in sound.

Digit	Letters	Explanation
1	d/t	Both have only one downstroke, and the letters sound similar.
2	n	N has two downstrokes.
3	m	M has three downstrokes.
4	r	R is the last letter of four, plus 4 and r have similarities.
5	l	In Roman numerals, L is 50.
6	j/g, sh, and soft ch	J has a lower loop, and g is similar to a 6 flipped over; sh and ch sound similar.
7	k, hard c, q	Capital K contains two 7s; hard c and q sound similar.
8	f/v, th	An old-fashioned f resembles an 8, and v sounds similar; th because of the ht in eight.
9	b/p	P can be seen as a mirror image of 9, and b sounds similar and also has a resemblance to a flipped 9.

In the system, it is the consonant sound that matters, not the spelling; for example, *action* would stand for 762, while *enough* would be 28 as the gh sounds like f.

If this memory system appeals to you, the first thing to do is to read through several times to make sure that it all makes sense. Don't be afraid to make changes to suit yourself. Mind trick expert Derren Brown uses f and v to represent the number five and ch/sh/j for eight. Once you are happy with your list, familiarize yourself with it and memorize it—read through slowly, write it out again, then turn the page over and check whether you can remember them all.

Now take things a step further and practice using it. A good place to start is by turning your PIN codes into words. Using the letters above, 9220 could become *bananas,* while 7510 could be *Celts.* Once you're happy with this, move on to longer telephone numbers. Remember to add in vowel sounds and the letters w, h, y to make several words or a sentence. The telephone number 0141 342 020 could become *Saturday morn snooze,* for instance, or you may find you prefer a sequence of images reflecting the person whose phone number it is.

The Major System works particularly effectively when combined with other mnemonic techniques, such as rhyming or memorable imagery, and with both the Peg and Loci systems. As always, the more familiar you are with the system and the more you use it, the more skillful you will become and the better your memory will be.

TIME AND CALENDARS

"We cross our bridges when we come to them and burn them behind us, with nothing to show for our progress except a memory of the smell of smoke, and a presumption that once our eyes watered."

Tom Stoppard

Time and calendars have inspired some of our best-known and oldest mnemonics, including one about the number of days in the months, which is familiar to most people. A few have known authors but most are of unknown origin.

CLOCKS FORWARD AND BACK

Spring forward, fall back.

We now think of fall as the American name for autumn, but in fact it was an Elizabethan term that must have traveled across the Atlantic with the Founding Fathers. This is widely used to help remember which way to reset the clocks for daylight saving time.

There is also another once popular rhyme:

> *Forward April, back September,*
> *That is all you need to remember.*

DAYS IN THE MONTH

Thirty days hath September,
April, June, and November.

All the rest have thirty-one
Except February alone,
Which has twenty-eight days clear
And twenty-nine in each leap year.

Alternatively, you can use your hands:
Excluding your thumbs, tap the knuckles and spaces in between so that January is high, February low, March high, April low. When you run out of knuckles on one hand, start again on the second with high August, low September, and so on. The months where you have tapped a low have fewer days than the high months, which all have thirty-one.

THE FOUR SEASONS

For clues to the official date when each season begins, remember that all start on the 20-something of the month and then count the number of vowels in each season's name.

Season	No. of Vowels	Start Date
sprIng	1	March 21
sUmmEr	2	June 22
AUtUmn	3	September 23
wIntEr	2	December 22

To help fix the months, remember that the shortest day—the start of winter—is just three days before Christmas and that the seasons change every quarter year, or every three months.

SIGNS OF THE ZODIAC

The zodiac is usually taken to refer to the annual cycle of twelve signs marking the sun's elliptic path. It is derived from ancient Babylonian and Greek astronomy and was certainly used in Roman times and is described in Ptolemy's *Almagest*, written in the second century AD. The zodiac remains the basis of the elyptic coordinate system that is still used in astronomy.

Think of this mnemonic for the names of all twelve signs in order:

A Timid Gray Cat Lay Very Low, Skulking Slowly,
Contemplating A Pigeon.

Aries, Taurus, Gemini, Cancer, Leo, Virgo, Libra, Scorpio, Sagittarius, Capricorn, Aquarius, Pisces.

Ebenezer Cobham Brewer (of *Brewer's Dictionary of Phrase and Fable* fame) wrote a verse describing the symbols for each constellation rather than the name in most cases. Again beginning with Aries in the spring:

> Our vernal signs the Ram begins,
> Then comes the Bull, in May the Twins;
> The Crab in June, next Leo shines,
> And Virgo ends the northern signs.
>
> The Balance brings autumnal fruits,
> The Scorpion stings, the Archer shoots;
> December's Goat brings wintry blast,
> Aquarius rain, the Fish comes last.

IDES AND NONES

Before the adoption of the Julian calendar in 46 BC, the Romans are believed to have used a lunar calendar, possibly based on a more ancient Greek version. This involved counting backward from three fixed points in the following month, the nones, the ides, and the kalends. This rhyme has helped classical scholars:

> In March, July, October, May,
> The ides are on the fifteenth day,
> The nones the seventh, but all besides
> Have two days less for nones and ides.

THE ALPHABET TECHNIQUE

Like the number/rhyme system, the Alphabet Technique is a pegword memory system using the letters of the alphabet in place of numbers. It works by creating images for each letter and then linking them to items on the list you want to remember. Because the alphabet is so ingrained in our minds, at its most basic, this technique can be a good way of learning longer lists in order and in a way that makes it obvious when anything is missing. It is more sophisticated than the number/rhyme system but rather more difficult to learn and can seem unnecessarily complicated. Tony Buzan, in his book *Use Your Perfect Memory*, suggests concentrating on the phonetic sound of the letter rather than the letter itself; so, for instance, the letter K is represented by a cake rather than a kite.

As with all such memory techniques, it is important that the images work for you, so don't be afraid to play around and change them.

Here is the image scheme that's most frequently used, but feel free to go with the picture that has the strongest connection for you:

A	Ace of spades	F	Effluent
B	Bee	G	Jeans
C	Sea	H	H-bomb
D	Diesel engine	I	Eye
E	Eagle	J	Jade

K	Cake	S	Eskimo
L	Elephant	T	Teapot
M	Empty	U	Unicycle
N	Entrance	V	Vehicle
O	Oboe	W	WC
P	Pea	X	X-ray
Q	Queue	Y	Wire
R	Ark	Z	Zulu

© *Use Your Perfect Memory*, Tony Buzan, BBC Worldwide Limited.

Take some time to assimilate these images for each letter until you are completely familiar with them. Next, you should try associating items on a list with each letter. At this point I should admit that this is not a technique that really works for me. I find that it takes me such a long time to think of imaginative but workable ways to link images to each letter that it's quicker just to learn the list by reading and rereading. But it really does work well for many people and experts.

Often quoted examples of the Alphabet Technique use the names of famous philosophers:

A—the Ace of spades stands for Freud: a smoking ace is lifted from a Frying pan where it has been well FRiED.

G—Jeans stands for Nietzsche: a worn pair of Jeans has a Knee showing through.

H—H-bomb recalls Kafka: a bomb explodes a dismal, gray official café.

THE BIBLE/SUNDAY SCHOOL

"Science without religion is lame, religion without science is blind."

ALBERT EINSTEIN

I can remember learning "Matthew, Mark, Luke, and John, bless the bed that I lie on" at Sunday School in what amounted to a Nissen hut left over from World War II. I know I was very young because the fairly small upright piano appeared huge to me then. In my mind the verse is completely tied up with the songs, "The wise man built his house upon the rock," and "I will make you fishers of men," except that at the time I heard it as "fishy an' men," which puzzled me.

The Twelve Disciples

The Ignatian *Faith and Life* manual sets them out like this, relying on the similarities between a handwritten script *J* and *I:*

Bartholomew
Andrew
Peter, Philip
Thomas, Thaddaeus (also known as Judas)
John, James, James, Judas Iscariot
Simon
Matthew

Or: Bart and John fill Tom's Mat
           With two Jams, two Juds, and two Simons.

And: This is the way the disciples run:
           Peter, Andrew, James and John,
           Philip and Bartholomew,
           Thomas next and Matthew, too,
           James the less and Judas the greater,
           Simon the Zealot and Judas the traitor.

You've probably noticed a certain discrepancy, as the names of the twelve vary among the Gospels. They are generally listed as:

Simon (named Peter by Jesus) and his brother Andrew,
    who were both fishermen
James and John, sons of Zebedee (given the name
    Boanerges, or Sons of Thunder), who were also
    fishermen
Philip
Bartholomew
Thomas (sometimes referred to as "doubting" Thomas)
Matthew the tax collector
James son of Alphaeus (the lesser James)
Simon the Cananaean, also known as the Zealot
Judas (the greater) son of James (according to Luke) or
    Thaddaeus (according to Matthew and Mark)
Judas Iscariot

The Books of the Bible

The Old Testament

There are thirty-nine books in the Old Testament, and there's no point in pretending there's an easy way to learn them all. But there is a poem of unknown age and origin that can really help if you enjoy rhyme; and if you want to practice any of the memory techniques, this is the ideal list to peg to the number/rhyme mnemonic or Major System.

The great Jehovah speaks to us
In **Genesis** and **Exodus;**
Leviticus and **Numbers** see,
Followed by **Deuteronomy.**
Joshua and **Judges** sweep the land,
Ruth gleans a sheaf with trembling hand;
Samuelx2 and numerous **Kings**x2 appear,
Whose **Chronicles**x2 we wondering hear.

Ezra and **Nehemiah** now,
Esther the beauteous mourner show,
Job speaks in sighs, David in **Psalms,**
The **Proverbs** teach us to scatter alms.

Ecclesiastes then comes on,
And the sweet **Song of Solomon.**
Isaiah, **Jeremiah** then
With **Lamentations** takes his pen.

Ezekiel, Daniel, Hosea's lyres,
Swell **Joel, Amos, Obadiah**'s.
Next **Jonah, Micah, Nahum** come,
And lofty **Habbakuk** finds room.

While **Zephaniah, Haggai** calls,
Rapt **Zechariah** builds his walls,
And **Malachi** with garments rent,
Concludes the ancient testament.

This sentence is an extra aid for the first five books:

God's Exalted Love Never Dies.

The Four Gospels

Many people will remember from childhood:

Matthew, Mark, Luke, and John,
Went to bed with their trousers on.

And the prayer:

Matthew, Mark, Luke, and John
Bless the bed that I lie on.
If I die before I wake,
I pray dear Lord my soul to take.

The Books of the New Testament

There are 27 books in the New Testament: think back to the 39 in the Old Testament, or usefully, the letters of *New* (3) and *Testament* (9) and simply multiply 3 by 9.

The books are usually broken into chunks with sentences to prompt your memory:

Matthew	Corinthians 1 and 2
Mark	Galatians
Luke	Ephesians
John	Philippians
Acts	Colossians
Romans	

Matthew, Mark, Luke, and John Act Rather too Corny at the General Electric Power Company.

Or assuming it's fairly easy to remember Matthew, Mark, Luke, John, Acts, you can then use:

Roosters Can Crow, Geese Eat Pop Corn, Turkeys Trot.

for Romans, Corinthians 1 and 2, Galatians, Ephesians, Philippians, Colossians, and Thessalonians 1 and 2 from the next section.

It's also useful to bear in mind that all the books beginning with a *T* come together in the New Testament:

Thessalonians 1 and 2
Timothy 1 and 2
Titus

Philemon
Hebrews

Then The Timothys Taught Titus Philemon's Hebrew.

James
Peter 1 and 2
John 1,2 and 3

Jude
Revelation

James, two Peters, three Johns, and one Jude found Revelation.

The Seven Deadly Sins

The named seven have changed and developed somewhat over the centuries, and if you look at Galatians chapter 5, you will find a much longer list. However, it is now usually agreed to be:

Wrath, Avarice, Gluttony, Sloth, Pride, Lust, Envy.

We All Gain Semi Professional Leaders Easily.

Or you can take each initial to make either WASP LEG or PAW LEGS.

The Virtues

The seven corresponding virtues are:

Humility, Charity, Kindness, Temperance, Chastity, Diligence, Patience.

Which can be remembered by:

Humorous Clare Kindly Takes Charge During Parties.

Or from 1 Corinthians 13:13 the four traditional Christian virtues of faith, hope, charity, and love, which are probably more easily remembered than the sentence:

Flowers Hopefully Chase Light.

There are also the fruits of the Spirit as outlined in Galatians 5:22–23:

> "But the fruit of the Spirit is love, joy, peace, patience, kindness, goodness, faithfulness, gentleness and self-control."

USING YOUR SENSES

"The smell and taste of things remain poised a long time, like souls bearing resiliently on tiny and almost impalpable drops of their essence, the immense edifice of memory."

MARCEL PROUST

There are three basic steps in the creation of memories: sensory memory, short-term memory, and long-term memory. Information is first absorbed by the sensory memory, which holds an exact copy but only for a few seconds. The information is then transferred to the short-term memory, which is sometimes more usefully called the working memory. It is this working memory that is sometimes disrupted in dyslexics, making it hard for them to process and assimilate lots of messages quickly. Psychologist George Miller calculates that the short-term memory can hold seven bits of information plus or minus two. "Bits" are basically units such as numbers, phrases, or words. The last stage involves the transfer of information into long-term memory, probably in the hippocampus, where it is organized for easy retrieval.

The senses are always involved to a degree in memory. Who hasn't caught a particular smell, such as newly mown grass, fresh coffee, or even sun screen, and been instantly transported to another time and place? Taste can do the same. Proust was not alone in his appreciation of a madeleine, and sound is just as compelling: when using the Loci System, many people find it improves their recall if they add distinct sound effects or music. But for some people, their senses add an extra element to the way they remember and recall information.

MEMORY AND COLOR

The American Psychological Society is just one organization that has reported on the influence of color on memory.

During a demonstration to show the limits of human memory, university students were read four lists of nine numbers. Afterward, most people could recall six, seven, or occasionally eight of the numbers in each list, but at the end of the class, about two hours later, one twenty-one-year-old could recall all four lists of digits. Not only that, but when paid a surprise visit two months later, she could still remember them perfectly.

Why was she able to recall the numbers so easily? For her, each number had a specific color or photism, and it was the colors that made the digits so easy to remember.

This ability is called "digit-color synesthesia," and in common with other synesthetes, this student's digit-color matchings did not change over time, and they happen automatically. These are now fairly well-documented phenomena, another famous case being that of the professional mnemonist Shereshevsky, in the mid-twentieth century, who was also a synesthete. After studying fifty digits for three minutes, he was able to remember them all even many years later.

MEMORY AND MUSIC

Learning to read music and play an instrument can help children improve their language skills and may even aid recovery in cases of memory loss following brain injury. Psychologists at the Chinese University in Hong Kong studied a group of schoolboys aged six to fifteen and found that those learning an instrument could recall significantly more words when tested than their nonmusical counterparts. The same results were found when the boys were retested after thirty minutes. It seems the longer the boys had been learning an instrument, the more words they remembered. Interestingly, the findings applied only to words, not images. The findings echoed an earlier study of girls where musical students out-performed the nonmusical by 16 percent in verbal tests.

SONGS AS MNEMONICS

There's no doubt that songs help you learn, sometimes even when you don't want to. Most people can remember words to songs they heard years ago, even when they dislike the song. Snatches of tunes play through your brain whether you want them to or not and are sometimes hard to shift.

At their most basic level, songs are a simple mnemonic device that helps you learn and memorize information. It seems they tap into a primitive part of our brain. Music prompts our memory for words, resonating with our ancient

roots. Music, song, and speech were always part of our com-
munication with one another, just as animals use sound and
song to communicate. It's easy to forget that long stories,
verses, and poems were learned by heart to be recited or sung
with ease at a time before print became commonplace and few
people could read. Speech and song are part of our oral and
aural tradition.

The rhymes and verses also naturally break material into
chunks that are easier for our brains to code and store. As
children we learn our first songs using rhyme and tunes to
help us remember.

Neurobiological research has established a close link
between the brain's hearing and emotional centers. Dr. Mark
Tramo, director of the Institute for Music and Brain Science at
Harvard, says, "The connectivity of the brain's auditory and
emotional systems underlie musical aesthetics," which helps
to explain why music has such a powerful effect on our minds
and memories.

We are constantly advised to create an image to establish an
emotional connection with the information we want to
remember. With music we don't need to try; the connection is
already there.

MEMORY, SMELL, AND TASTE

"For the sense of smell, almost more than any other, has the power to recall memories and it is a pity that you use it so little."

RACHEL CARSON

Scents and tastes instantly evoke a wave of memories that can influence our mood and performance. From an evolutionary perspective, these two senses are our most important; and they link directly to the most primitive part of our brain, the home of instinct and memory. As with all mammals, it is through smell and taste that we recognize food and poison— those things that will nourish us and those that will make us ill—functions fundamental to our basic survival.

Humans have around a thousand scent receptors or sensors in their noses and can identify something like ten thousand different smells. Each sensor recognizes several smells, and in turn a single smell is recognized by several different receptors. At Harvard, Associate Professor Linda Buck likens this system to individual letters being used in various combinations to make words.

The scent molecule enters the nose, where it is recognized by scent receptors that send signals to the olfactory bulb in the brain, just above the eyes. From there, signals are sent to both the limbic system and the olfactory part of the cortex. The limbic system is the primitive part of the brain so closely

CREATING
A MEMORABLE RANDOM PASSWORD

It's so easy to fall into the habit of using the same password for everything, which, if you believe all the warnings, can leave you vulnerable to identity fraud.

To choose a password that appears completely random but is also easy to remember, try this: make up a sentence that you commit to memory and simply use the first letter of each word as your password. It is also easy to build numbers into it. For example:

I Watched The Northern Lights In September 08 In Lapland.

Which gives you an 11-digit password including two numbers: IWTNLIS08IL

associated with memory, feelings, and behavior that it is sometimes called the "emotional" brain. The cortex is in the outer part of the brain that is concerned with conscious thought. The signals also travel to the taste sensory cortex to create a sense of taste.

Although sensory neurons survive for only about two months, smells and tastes can bring back distant memories. This is because new olfactory neurons are constantly generated, and signals from particular receptors always go to the same place.

Trygg Engen, a psychologist at Brown University, states that smells act as "index keys" to quickly recall certain memories in our brain, which is why smell and taste can trigger more instant and powerful memories than either sight or hearing.

We also have conditioned responses to certain smells and flavors. When you first smell or taste something new, you link it with a particular event or person and the brain forges a link. Often these are childhood memories, because we mainly come across new scents and tastes when we are young.

MATH
AND NUMBERS

*"Do not worry about your difficulties
in mathematics. I can assure you mine
are still greater."*

ALBERT EINSTEIN

It's only since I left school and didn't need to worry about math tests and exams anymore that I began to appreciate the patterns in numbers and realize that there really are symmetry and logic to math. It is also only recently that I discovered that there are many helpful tricks for remembering the rules.

PI

The value of Pi is the ratio of the circumference to the diameter of a circle, hence the equation Area = Pi x r squared. There are various sentences using words of different lengths to represent each digit.

The first eight decimal places of Pi:

3.14159266

May I have a large container of coffee?

To thirteen places:

3.141592653589

See, I have a rhyme assisting my feeble brain its tasks sometimes resisting.

And to thirty-one places:

3.1415926535897932384626433833279

Now I, even I, would
Celebrate
In rhymes unapt, the great
Immortal Syracusan, rivaled
Nevermore,
Who in his wondrous lore,
Passed on before,
Left men his guidance
How to circles mensurate.

Or:

Sir, I send a rhyme excelling
In sacred truth and rigid spelling
Numerical sprites elucidate
For me the lexicon's full weight
If nature gain, who can complain
Tho' Doc Johnson fulminate.

This is a mnemonic limerick that not only helps you remember Pi to five decimal places, but also reminds you how to calculate the circumference of a circle:

If you cross a circle with a line
Which hits the center and runs from spine to spine
And the line's length is C
The circumference will be C times 3.14159.

PRIME NUMBERS

Prime numbers are numbers that can only be divided by 1 and themselves. Working on the same principle as the Pi mnemonics, count the letters of each word in the following sentence for the first seven prime numbers:

In the early morning, astronomers spiritualized nonmathematicians.

2 3 5 7 11 13 17

The hundredth prime number is 541 and the thousandth, 7,919.

THE METRIC SYSTEM

Kilometer hectometer decameter meter decimeter
centimeter millimeter
King Hector Died Miserable Death—
Caught Measles.

This can be slightly adapted as:

King Hector Doesn't Usually Drink Cold Milk.

For:

Kilo	1000	Deci	0.1
Hecto	100	Centi	0.01
Deca	10	Milli	0.001
Units	1		

WEIGHTS AND MEASURES

The weight of water in a U.S. pint is 16 fluid ounces:

A pint's a pound
In the world around.

It's sometimes useful to remember that a UK pint is 20 fluid ounces:

A pint of water
Weighs a pound and a quarter.

And to remember the number of liters in a U.S. pint:

A pint of water
Is just over a quarter

1 pint = 0.473176 liters, to be exact

CALCULUS

The positive quadrants:
All Sine Tangent Cosine
All students take calculus.

TRIGONOMETRY

Tan=opposite/adjacent
The old Arab   Cos=adjacent/hypotenuse
           carried a heavy   Sine=opp/hypotenuse
                       sack of hay.

SOHCAHTOA

To remember the three main trigonometric functions:

For Sine you divide Opposite side over Hypotenuse;
for Cosine you divide Adjacent side over Hypotenuse;
for Tangent you divide Opposite side over Adjacent side.

And to remember SOHCAHTOA:

Some Old Horse
Caught A Horse
Taking Oats Away

Or:

Silly Old Harry
Caught A Herring
Trawling Off America

PYTHAGORAS'S THEOREM

The theorem allows pupils to find the length of the third side of a right-angled triangle given the lengths of the other two sides:

"In a right-angled triangle the square of the hypotenuse is equal to the sum of the square of the other two sides."

Or you may find it easier to remember as:

The squaw on the hippopotamus is equal to the sum of the squaws on the other two hides.

MATHEMATICAL PROBLEMS

Parenthesis Exponents Multipliers Dividers
Adders Subtractors
Please Excuse My Dear
aunt Sally.

That is the order in which you should tackle a math problem.

Division

Smaller unit into a Larger? Remember they Divide:

Snails Love Dessert.

Larger unit into a Smaller? Remember they will Multiply:

Llamas Slurp Milk.

1 over 7

is .14 28 57
Just learn one,
The others are given.

Dividing by Fractions

Just remember this little rhyme:

The number you're dividing by,
Turn upside down and multiply.

So 8/1/2 become 8 x 2/1 = 16

Long Division

The order of operations—Divide, Multiply, Subtract, Compare, Remainder—can be remembered by:

Does Mcdonald's Sell Cheeseburgers Raw?

Or you may prefer:

Dad, Mum, Sister, and Brother, for

Divide, Multiply, Subtract, and Bring Down.

Multiplication

Minus times minus is plus,
The reason for this we need not discuss.

Even times even is even,
Even times odd is even,
But odd times odd is always odd.

Numerator over the Denominator

Nice Dog.

Borrowing in Subtraction

Bigger bottom better borrow.

TIMES TABLES

I went to school at a time when it was still common practice to chant times tables every day out loud in class. And I have to say, the method worked with me; well, at least I can usually get to the right answer even if it means chanting a few numbers, usually starting from 5 times something to reach it. As it turned out, this was also the method that worked for my daughter, who found anything involving numbers an immediate off switch. For a time, reciting one of the tables, chanting it aloud in a singsong fashion, was part of our daily walk to school. We'd begin at the park gate and continue until we reached a particular tree that marked the end of that day's session. Kept short, often repeated, and made as much fun as possible, it didn't seem a chore. But there are also other ways to help learning.

One of the best ways to prompt memory is to look for the patterns in the times tables.

2 Times

This is really just a case of doubling the number you are multiplying by:

$2 \times 2 = 4, 2 \times 3 = 6, 2 \times 4 = 8, 2 \times 5 = 10, 2 \times 6 = 12$, and so on.

And once you know your 2 times table, you also know $3 \times 2, 4 \times 2$, etc., so you are beginning to learn other tables.

3 Times

If you add the digits in the 3 times table, they always make 3 or a multiple of 3:

3 6 9 12 15 18 21 24 27 30 33 36

5 Times

The 5 times table alternately ends in 0 or 5, and it is also always half of 10 times a number, which is the easiest times table of all to learn.

6 Times

When multiplying 6 by an even number, just remember that both the even number and the answer end in the same digit:

6 x 2 = 12, 6x 4 = 24, 6 x 6 = 36, 6 x 8 = 48

8 Times

Beginning with 8, the units always descend in 2s throughout this table:

8 16 24 32 40 48 56 64 72 80 88 96

9 Times

This times table contains several distinct patterns:

9 18 27 36 45 54 63 72 81 90 99 108

As the tens go up, the units go down—9, 8, 7, etc. Another prompt is the fact that the tens number is always one less than the number you are multiplying by, so:

$9 \times 2 = 18, 9 \times 5 = 45, 7 \times 9 = 63, 9 \times 9 = 81$

And if you add up the digits, they always make 9, with the exception of 9+9:

1+8, 2+7, 3+6, 4+5, 9+0, 1+8

10 Times
The simplest to remember because all you have to do is take the number you are multiplying by and add a zero:

20 30 40 50 60 70 80 90 100 110 120

11 Times
This is fairly easy once you've noted that you just put two digits of the number you are multiplying by together:

$11 \times 2 = 22, 11 \times 3 = 33, 11 \times 4 = 44$, and so on until
11×10—remember the 10 times table and add a zero—110
$11 \times 11 = 121$
$11 \times 12 = 132$

12 Times

If you have worked through all the tables, once you have reached 12 x, you have already covered it and the only new number is:

12 X 12 = 144

Working on the principle that the more connections you can make the more routes you have to remember, it's also useful to think that 12 is 10 x plus 2 x.

To help yourself further you can also draw out a multiplication square:

	1	2	3	4	5	6	7	8	9	10	11	12
1	1	2	3	4	5	6	7	8	9	10	11	12
2	2	4	6	8	10	12	14	16	18	20	22	24
3	3	6	9	12	15	18	21	24	27	30	33	36
4	4	8	12	16	20	24	28	32	36	40	44	48
5	5	10	15	20	25	30	35	40	45	50	55	60
6	6	12	18	24	30	36	42	48	54	60	66	72
7	7	14	21	28	35	42	49	56	63	70	77	84
8	8	16	24	32	40	48	56	64	72	80	88	96
9	9	18	27	36	45	54	63	72	81	90	99	108
10	10	20	30	40	50	60	70	80	90	100	110	120
11	11	22	33	44	55	66	77	88	99	110	121	132
12	12	24	36	48	60	72	84	96	108	120	132	144

This helps to fix the patterns in your mind and is a useful quick reference when needed!

SLEEP AND MEMORY

*"Early to bed and early to rise makes a man
healthy, wealthy and wise."*

BENJAMIN FRANKLIN

Scientists now believe that sleep is essential for memory consolidation, the process by which a memory is coded and fixed so that it can be retrieved and used, for instance in an exam.

Several cleverly designed sleep deprivation experiments, including one at Harvard Medical School, have shown that if people did not sleep within thirty hours of studying, their memory of what they had tried to learn would be impaired. It appears that both slow wave and REM sleep, which occur late in the sleep cycle, are necessary for the maximum improvement in performance and that there is a sequential process for memory consolidation at work. During REM sleep the brain and body become active, heart rate and blood pressure increase, and there is characteristic eye shuddering or rapid eye movements. Episodes last anywhere from eleven to twenty-five minutes, and these are the periods of sleep that are most associated with dreaming. It is possible that the memories we don't think about are relived during REM sleep, in the form of dreams, so that we can recall them when needed.

Dr. Andrew Tilley of the University of Queensland said, "It looks like there's a window of opportunity following a learning episode in which sleep needs to occur in order for it to have beneficial effects on memory and that the window shuts around twenty-six to thirty hours."

Further studies have also shown that sleep deprivation, particularly a lack of REM sleep, leads to poor performance in memory recall or logical tests and that memory loss occurs if a student is deprived of sleep on the two nights following a study session: this is particularly linked to the first and last two periods of REM sleep. Interestingly, REM density, or the number of rapid eye movements per minute, has been found to increase for several nights after intense studying.

Not all scientists agree that there is a link between sleep and memory. Some argue that far from consolidating memories during REM episodes and dreams, the brain is actually using this time to dispose of unwanted material to avoid overload.

STUDYING FOR EXAMS

*"To accomplish great things,
we must dream as well as act."*

ANATOLE FRANCE

It seems that Granny might have been right when she advised a "good night's sleep" and warned "If you don't know it by now, you never will" when you were frantically cramming at the last minute for an exam.

BIOLOGY

"I've a grand memory for forgetting."

Robert Louis Stevenson

Scientists generally, but medical students in particular, have come up with the most incredible number of mnemonics for the names of bones and biochemical reactions. There are far too many to include here, but the sheer volume and inventiveness are impressive. Here are just a few that may prove useful at some point.

TAXONOMIC CLASSIFICATIONS

Taxonomy is the science and practice of classification, and in biological terms this refers to the hierarchical classification of organisms.

Kings Play Chess On Fridays Generally Speaking and
Katie Puts Cake On Fred's Good Shirt

are just two examples of an old mnemonic for the division of animals into seven groups:

Kingdom, Phylum, Class, Order, Family, Genus, Species.

Others include:

Kings Play Chess On Fine Green Silk.

Kings Play Chess on Fine Grained Sand.
Kangaroos Pounce Cheekily On Fred's Green Sauce.
Kids Playing Catch On Freeways Go Splat.
Kryptonite Promotes Casualty Overwhelmingly For Great
    Superman.

And there are many, many others.

While zoologists use the word *phylum,* botanists substitute the term *division,* so a better version for any botanist is:

King David Comes Over For Great Spaghetti.

There are also subdivisions within these groups, and the complete Linnaean order of classification is:

Kingdom	Family
Subkingdom	Subfamily
	Tribe
Phylum	
Subphylum	Genus
Superclass	Subgenus
Class	Species
Subclass	Subspecies
Infraclass	
Cohort	
Superorder	
Order	
Suborder	
Superfamily	

Man's Taxonomy
All Chaperones Must Previously Have Had Sex.

Animalia, Chordata, Mammalia, Primata, Hominidae, Homo Sapiens.

THE SEVEN ACTIVITIES OF ALL LIVING THINGS

There are seven activities common to all living things in the cycle of life:

Movement
Respiration
Sensitivity
Growth
Reproduction
Excretion
Nutrition

Generations of school children have been taught to remember them by the acronym

MRS. GREN

Or if you choose to call *Sensitivity Excitability,* you have

MR. GREEN

KREBS CYCLE

The Krebs Cycle was first recognized by the German bio-chemist Hans Adolph Krebs in 1937. It is also known as the tri-carboxylic acid cycle (TCA), or citric acid cycle, and refers to a complex series of chemical reactions in all cells that utilize oxygen in their respiration process. It is the metabolic pathway involved in the chemical conversion of carbohydrates, proteins, and fats into carbon dioxide and water to generate usuable energy.

The eight stages are:

Citrate, Isocitrate, Ketoglutarate, Succinyl, Succinate, Fumarate, Malate, Oxaloacetate.

I have found two mnemonic sentences to remember them:

Can Intelligent Karen Solve Some Foreign Mafia Operations?

and

Cindy Is Kinky So She Fornicates More Often.

VERTEBRATE ANIMAL CLASSIFICATIONS

An easy way to remember the five classes is:

FARM B

Fish, Amphibians, Reptiles, Mammals, Birds.

LICHEN

Lichen are made up of algae and fungi:

She was all gal (algae) and he was a fun guy (fungi).
They took a likin' (lichen) to each other.

SEDGES, RUSHES, AND GRASSES

To tell which is which:

Sedges have edges,
Rushes are round,
Grasses are hollow right down to the ground.

And:

Sedges have edges,
Rushes are round,
And grasses like asses have holes.

THE BODY

The Human Skeleton

Tibia and Fibula

For the position, remember: the Fibula is lateral.
And:

The Tibia is thick like a tuba,
The Fibula is thin like a flute.

Carpal Bones

The carpal bones are actually part of the wrist rather than the hand, allowing the joint to move and rotate. It is the bones of the metacarpus that are part of the hand.

Senior Lecturers Try Positions That They Can't Handle, or
Stop Letting Those People Touch That Cadaver's Hand.

These give the eight carpal bones in order of position:

Scaphoid, Lunate, Triquetrum, Pisiform, Trapezium, Trapezoid, Capitate, Hamate.

Positions of the Trapezium and Trapezoid:

The Trapez**ium** is by the th**um**b, the Trapez**oid** is by its **side**.

The **H**amate has the **H**ook.

A rather more complicated version with more prompts for each bone is:

The Boat sailed to the Moon with Three PEAs in a rOw.
At the wheel was Captain Hook.

Boat is Scaphoid.
Moon is Lunate.
Three is Triquetrum (also known as triquetral bone).
Peas is Pisiform.
Stress the EA sound in Peas for Trapezium.
Row is Trapezoid.

Captain is Capitate (the largest of the bones and at the
center of the wrist).

Hook is Hamate.

Facial Bones

Virgil Cannot Now Make My Pet Zebra Laugh.

Vomer, Conchae, Nasal, Maxilla, Mandible, Palatine,
Zygomatic, Lacrimal.

Cranial or Skull Bones

Fraternity Parties Occasionally Teach Spartan Etiquette.

This gives the first two letters of each bone:

Frontal, Parietal, Occipital, Temporal, Sphenoid,
Ethmoid.

Or you may prefer STEP OF(f my skull) or PEST OF 6.

The Bones of the Arm and Shoulder

*Some Crooks Have Underestimated Royal Canadian Mounted
Police.*

This list gives the bones in order:

Scapula, Clavicle, Humerus, Ulna, Radius, Carpals,
Metacarpals, Phalanges.

The Leg Bones

Help Five Police To Find Ten Missing Prisoners.

In order:

Hip, Femur, Patella, Tibia, Fibula, Tarsals, Metarsals, Phalanges.

Vertebrae of the Spinal Column

Clever Dick Likes Sugar Candy.

Cervical, Dorsal (which is also known as Thoracic), Lumbar, Sacrum, Coccyx.

Ossification

Ossification is the normal process of bone formation. Initially, a child's skeleton is largely composed of relatively soft cartilage that gradually develops into bones. Anatomists can remember the ages at which different bones harden:

Every Potential Anatomist Should Know When (bones ossify).
Elbow—16 years
Pelvis—17 years
Ankle—17 years
Shoulder—18 years
Knee—18 years
Wrist—19 years

The Inner Ear Bones

Describing the shape and position of the bones working inward:

> *Take a hammer*—Malleus
> *Hit an Indian elephant*—Incus
> *Which puts its foot in a stirrup*—Stapes

Another option is **Ma**iling **In**cludes **Sta**mps.

THE TWELVE CRANIAL NERVES

There are twelve pairs of cranial nerves, all with distinct functions:

	Nerve	*Function*
I	Olfactory	Smell
II	Optic	Vision
III	Oculomotor	Movement of eyelid and eyeball
IV	Trochlear	Turns eye downward and laterally
V	Trigeminal	Chewing, touch, and pain in face and mouth
VI	Abducens	Turns eye laterally

	Nerve	Function
VII	Facial	Controls most facial expressions, secretion of tears and saliva, taste
VIII	Auditory (or Vestibulocochlear)	Hearing and sense of equilibrium
IX	Glossopharyngeal	Taste, senses carotid blood pressure
X	Vagus	Senses aortic blood pressure, slows heart rate, stimulates digestive organs, taste
XI	Spinal Accessory	Swallowing movements, controls sternocleido-mastoid and trapezius
XII	Hypoglossal	Controls tongue movements

Medical students have devised a large number of mnemonics to help them remember these. One of the most used (and cleanest) is:

On Old Olympus's Towering Top, A Finn and German Viewed Some Hops.

And to remember whether a nerve is sensory (s), motor (m),

or both (b), apply the first letter of the words of this twelve-word sentence to the correspondingly numbered nerve:

Some Say Marry Money But My Brother Says
Big Boobs Matter More!

WHITE BLOOD CELLS

Nobody Likes My Educational Background.

Which gives in order of decreasing numbers:

Neutrophils
Lymphocytes
Monocytes
Eosinophils
Basophils

CELL CYCLE

Go Sally Go! Make Children!

G_1, S, G_2, M, C.

Or expressed more fully:

Growth phase 1, DNA Synthesis (replication),
Growth phase 2, Mitosis, Cytokinesis.

MITOSIS

People Meet And Talk, or

Prophase, Metaphase, Anaphase, Telophase.

For the five stages of cell division in Mitosis:

Interphase, Prophase, Metphase, Anaphase, Telophase,

I Painted My Attic Today.

EIGHT ESSENTIAL AMINO ACIDS

I Like To Teach My Vets Lumbar Puncture.

Isoleucine, Leucine, Threonine, Tryptophan, Methionine, Valine, Lysine, Phenylalanine.

ANIMALS

Elephants

What's the difference between an African and an Indian elephant?

It sounds like the beginning of a joke, but there are a number of differences. The most obvious is that the African elephant is not only larger, but it also has bigger ears.

India's big and its elephant there features,
But Africa's bigger with much bigger creatures.

And:

India's big but Africa's bigger,
The same as their elephants—easy to figure.

Alongside the difference in ear size, there is also a difference in shape. As a rough guide, African elephants' ears usually resemble the outline of Africa with a definite extra curve at the top, while Indian elephants' ears look more like the triangular shape of India.

ELEPHANT FACTS

· Both African and Indian elephants can smell water more than 3 miles away.

· Elephants are the only mammals unable to jump. Although they have knees, they weigh too much.

· Elephants are strong swimmers.

· They can communicate over long distances through low-frequency sound that they pick up through the sensitive skin of their trunks and feet.

· Their gestation period is 22 months, the longest of any land animal, and calves weigh about 250 pounds.

· Prehistoric ancestors include hairy mammoths that may have survived until as recently as 2000 BC in their dwarf forms.

· Small prehistoric elephants the size of large pigs lived on the island of Crete during the Pleistocene epoch.

· They are a symbol of wisdom in Asia, where they are famed for their memory and intelligence.

· They have long been working animals, particularly in the logging industry in Asia, although it is usually females that are domesticated and tamed.

· War elephants were frequently used by armies in India, and later China and the Persian and Greek empires. They were famously taken across the Alps by Hannibal, and a charging elephant could wreak havoc among infantry and cavalry soldiers.

- "An elephant never forgets." Elephants follow the same paths and seem to pass genetic memories of routes and places on through the generations. Each clan also has its own burial ground, and it will help ailing members return there. They develop strong, lasting relationships with one another and indeed with humans

African Elephants

- Both males and females have external tusks.
- They are generally less hairy than Indian (or Asian) elephants.
- African elephants have two "fingers" at the tips of their trunks.
- There are two types of African elephant—bush or savannah and forest—and recent evidence has suggested that they may be separate species, although this has yet to be universally accepted.
- Bush elephants are bigger. Males can reach more than 13 feet at the shoulder and can weigh between 7,700 pounds and a staggering 26,500 pounds.
- Bush elephants are found in the savannah area south of the Sahara, ranging over grasslands, marshes, and lakeshores.
- The forest elephant tends to be smaller and rounder, with thinner, straighter tusks.
- Forest elephants are found in the dense rain forests of central Asia and Africa, although they do overlap with savannah territories.

· Male forest elephants stand up to 10 feet tall at the shoulder and weigh up to 9,900 pounds.

· For much of the twentieth century, African elephant populations were in decline largely because of poaching.

· In 2007 it was estimated that there were between 470,000 and 690,000 elephants in the wild, although the true figure is hard to determine. It does seem that the largest populations, found in southern and eastern Africa, have been stable or steadily increasing since the 1990s.

· African elephants are faster and more powerful than their Indian cousins and far more difficult to train.

Indian or Asian Elephants

· Only males have tusks; the females' are so small they are hardly visible.

· They have only one "finger" at the tips of their trunks.

· Large males can be more than 9 feet tall and weigh up to 11,900 pounds.

· White, or albino, elephants are considered sacred in Burma and Thailand.

· It is estimated that there are between 38,000 and 53,000 wild elephants and up to 15,300 domesticated elephants in Asia.

· Populations have declined but rather more gradually than those of African elephants, due mainly to poaching and loss of natural habitat.

Camels

There are two main species of camel: the Bactrian camel, which still exists in the wild in the colder regions of central Asia, and the Arabian dromedary camel, which is lighter and faster, adapted to the dry desert areas of western Asia and sub-Saharan Africa. Dromedaries were domesticated long ago and are extinct as a wild species.

To remember the obvious difference between the two:

A Bactrian camel has two humps like a B,
While a dromedary has one hump just like a D.

White and Black Rhinoceros

The names are confusing because they cannot really be distinguished by color. "White" was a mistranslation of the Dutch word *weit,* meaning "wide."

To tell them apart, think white—wide, because the white rhino has a wide square snout, while the black rhino has a tapering triangular snout.

CAMEL FACTS

· Roughly 90 percent of the world's 14 million camels are dromedaries.

· There are an estimated 1.4 million Bactrian camels, with around 1,000 living wild in the Gobi Desert.

· Surprisingly, there are up to 700,000 feral dromedaries in central Australia, thought to be descendants of escaped transport camels introduced by Afghans in the nineteenth and early twentieth centuries.

· An adult stands about 6 feet at the shoulder and 7 feet to the top of the hump.

· Dromedary camels can reach speeds of 40 miles per hour in short bursts, with sustained speeds of 25 miles per hour.

· Both dromedaries and Bactrians are related to South American llamas, vicunas, and alpacas.

· Fossils suggest camels evolved in North America during the Paleogene period and later spread to Asia.

· Average life expectancy is forty to fifty years.

· While it's said that elephants never forget, it's also claimed that camels never forget an injury.

RHINOCEROS FACTS

· Black rhinos are 4.6–5.6 feet tall at the shoulder and are up to 12 feet in length. They typically weigh between 1,760 and 3,000 pounds, with the females smaller than the males.

· They have two horns made of keratin; the longest sits at

the front of the nose and is usually about 1.60 feet long, although they are occasionally much longer.

· Black rhinos' color depends on the local soil, and they are not usually black.

· There are four subspecies of black rhinoceros, and in July 2006 the World Conservation Union declared the western black rhino extinct, with only a handful remaining in captivity.

· The black rhino's tapered prehensile lip is used for grasping twigs and leaves, while the white rhino's square snout is suited to eating grass.

· Both have very poor eyesight but excellent hearing and sense of smell. They have been known to charge tree trunks by mistake when they feel threatened.

· White rhinos are larger generally and also have larger ears and skulls as well as a distinct hump on the neck.

· White rhinos are savannah-dwelling grazers; black rhinos live in forest and scrub. Black rhinos are classified as endangered; white as "vulnerable."

· Rhinoceros date from the Miocene epoch.

· White rhinos are more gregarious, and both have an extensive "vocabulary" of bellows, grunts, growls, squeaks, and snorts.

· In spite of its bulk, the rhinoceros is very agile and can reach speeds of up to 30 miles per hour.

· They have a reputation for being bad-tempered, particularly in regions where they have been disturbed.

CHEMISTRY

"We are able to find everything in our memory which is like a dispensary or chemical laboratory in which chance steers our hand sometimes to a soothing drug and sometimes to a dangerous poison."

MARCEL PROUST.

Somehow I missed out on all but the most basic tuition in chemistry at school, but I find that I now know parts of the periodic table of elements entirely thanks to Tom Lehrer's song. Written in the 1950s, it is set to a version of Gilbert and Sullivan's "I Am the Very Model of a Modern Major General," from *The Pirates of Penzance*. Once you've heard it a few times, it tends to stick. If you're unfamiliar with it, you can find Lehrer's original plus various other versions on YouTube.

PERIODIC TABLE OF ELEMENTS

There's antimony, arsenic, aluminium, selenium,
And hydrogen and oxygen and nitrogen and rhenium
And nickel, neodymium, neptunium, germanium,
And iron, americium, ruthenium, uranium,
Europium, zirconium, lutetium, vanadium
And lanthanum and osmium and astatine and radium
And gold, protactinium and indium and gallium
And iodine and thorium and thulium and thallium.

There's yttrium, ytterbium, actinium, rubidium
And boron, gadolinium, niobium, iridium,

And strontium and silicon and silver and samarium,
And bismuth, bromine, lithium, beryllium and barium.

There's holmium and helium and hafnium and erbium
And phosphorus and francium and fluorine and terbium
And manganese and mercury, molybdenum, magnesium,
Dysprosium and scandium and cerium and cesium
And lead, praseodymium, and platinum, plutonium,
Palladium, promethium, potassium, polonium,
Tantalum, technetium, titanium, tellurium,
And cadmium and calcium and chromium and curium.

There's sulphur, californium and fermium, berkelium
And also mendelevium, einsteinium and nobelium
And argon, krypton, neon, radon, xenon, zinc and rhodium
And chlorine, carbon, cobalt, copper,
Tungsten, tin and sodium.

These are the only ones of which the news has come to
    Harvard,
And there may be many others but they haven't been
    discovered.

THE PERIODIC TABLE

The table is generally accredited to the Russian chemist Dmitri Mendeleev in 1869. It is designed to illustrate recurring or periodic trends in the properties of the elements. As new elements and theories explaining chemical behavior have been developed, the table has been adapted and extended.

The elements are set in order of their atomic weights beginning with the lightest, which is hydrogen. It follows Mendeleev's periodic law stating, "The properties of the elements are in periodic dependence upon their atomic weights."

Since its invention, the Periodic Table has been widely used in all areas of science and engineering.

RARE GASES

Rare gases form Group O in the Periodic Table and are listed in order of atomic weight:

He—Helium, Ne—Neon, A—Argon, Kr—Krypton,
Xe—Xenon, Rn—Radon.

These can be remembered by:

HEaven NEver Asked KRiegspiel's eXtra ReNt.

OXIDATION

To remind yourself that Oxidation is Loss and Reduction is Gain in the electron transfer chain, just think of:

OIL RIG

Or:

LEO the lion goes GER.

Lose Electrons = Oxidation
Gain Electrons = Reduction

And:

ORE

Oxidation is Removal of Electrons.

MIXING ACIDS AND WATER

*Add acid to water
Just as you oughta.*

BIOCHEMICAL PATHWAYS

Aldohexoses, which are monosaccharide sugars, can be remembered by a mnemonic said to have been thought up by the chemist Emil Fisher:

All Atruists Gladly Make Gum in Gallon Tanks.

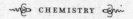
Allose, Altros, Glucose, Mannose, Gulose, Idose, Galactose, Tallose.

MEMORY TIPS OF A GRAND MASTER

Ed Cooke is a memory grand master. He has featured in the world memory championships top ten for the last six years and is still only twenty-six. He recently advised on how to learn verses in the national poetry recital competition for primary school children.

· He firmly believes that everyone is good at remembering something.
· The key is to be interested and motivated.
· And memory works best if you can make an emotional connection, which is one of the reasons why music can be so helpful: it immediately channels the emotional part of your brain.
· Think about how much you do remember. He points out that there is less information in a book, for example, than in your knowledge of what's in your home. Yet you don't even think about how you remember all that.
· When meeting someone, take an interest in them and repeat their name to yourself.
· We also remember the books we've read, the films we've watched, and the CDs we have listened to.

· Don't underestimate your memory. He recalls, "In an experiment they showed a group of people eighteen hundred photos and then tested them again after various lengths of time. Even twenty years later they were able to select a photo they had seen from one they hadn't. There is a colossal amount of information stored away."

· When teaching children to learn poems, find ways to make the words as vivid as possible and provide landmarks in the structure.

· Use your imagination to create interest and an emotional response to what you are trying to memorize.

· Age doesn't have to limit your brain power. Keep your expectations of yourself high. Everyone's forgetful sometimes; it's not just old age.

PHYSICS

"Science may set limits to knowledge but should not set limits to imagination."

BERTRAND RUSSELL

A knowledge of physics is fundamental to our understanding of the world and universe, and the laws that govern our existence. Included here are just a few of the more famous rules and theories.

EINSTEIN'S THEORY OF RELATIVITY AND THE SPEED OF LIGHT

Albert Einstein was one of the greatest physicists the world has known. His theory of relativity, put forward in the early part of the twentieth century, is one of the most significant scientific advances. It recognizes that the speed of light in a vacuum is constant. Which means that objects traveling close to the speed of light will appear to an observer on earth to move slower and shorten in length. The theory also gave rise to the famous equation:

$$E = mc^2$$

revealing the equivalence of mass and energy.

When applied to gravitational fields, the theory suggests the curve space-time continuum depicting the dimensions of space and time as a two-dimensional surface where large objects create dips in the surface.

The speed of light is always 299,792,458 meters per second, which can be worked out by using the number of characters in a word to equal a digit:

As Einstein's equations validly predicted, we hold speed constant.

THE ELECTROMAGNETIC SPECTRUM

Cary Grant eXpects Unanimous Votes In Movie Reviews Tonight helps to recall:

Cosmic, Gamma, X-rays, Ultraviolet, Visible, Infrared, Microwave, Radio, Television.

FLEMING'S RULE

Fleming's left-hand rule for electric motors shows the direction of the thrust on a conductor carrying a current in a magnetic field.

Hold the left hand with the thumb, index, and middle fingers at right angles.

- The **Thumb** represents the direction of **Thrust** or Motion.
- The **First** finger represents the direction of the **Field**.
- The se**Cond** finger represents the direction of the **Current** from positive to negative.

Fleming's right-hand rule for generators (or dynamos) shows

the direction of induced current flow when a conductor moves in a magnetic field.

Hold the right hand with the thumb, index, and middle fingers at right angles.

· The ThuMb represents the direction of Motion of the conductor.
· The First finger represents the direction of the Field.
· The seCond represents the induced or generated Current from positive to negative.

For both you can also use FBI as an acronym for:

Force, which is the thumb;
B, the magnetic field represented by the first finger;
I, the direction of the current, represented by the second finger.

To remember whether to use the left or right hand:

M is for Mum and for Motors.
D is for Dad and for Dynamos.
Dad is always right.

OHM'S LAW

Discovered by Georg Ohm in 1827, the law shows the relationship between voltage (V), current in amps (A), and resistance (R). It can be expressed in three ways:

V = A x R, A = V/R, R = V/A

To remember these set out a triangle:

$$V$$

$$A \quad R$$

· To calculate Voltage V, cover the V. This leaves A R, so the equation is V = A x R.
· To calculate Current A, cover the A. This leaves V over R, so the equation is A = V/R.
· To calculate Resistence R, cover the R. This leaves V over A, so the equation is R = V/A.

RAINBOWS AND THE COLOR SPECTRUM

The order of the seven colors of the light spectrum, as seen so clearly in rainbows, is:

Red, Orange, Yellow, Green, Blue, Indigo, Violet.

Scientists, often use:

ROY G. BIV

I have to say, I much prefer:

Richard Of York Gave Battle In Vain.

This refers to the infamous King Richard III of Great Britain.

PRIMARY AND SECONDARY COLORS

The primary colors of light are blue, green, and red; when combined, these three make total color, which is white light.

The secondary colors of yellow, magenta, and cyan are used to make most other shades. They are also called subtractive colors because when they are combined they each absorb one primary color of light—so there is no light left to see.

The sentence used to remember this is:

Better Get Ready When
Your Mistress Comes Back.

Blue+Green+Red = White
Yellow+Magenta+Cyan = Black

FORCE AND MOTION

Distance, Speed, and Velocity.

Distance is the measure of how far an object has traveled or how far away it is. It is the same as length and is measured in meters.

Speed is a measure of how fast an object is traveling and is measured in meters per second.

Velocity also measures how fast an object is moving in meters per second, but it differs from speed in that velocity measures speed in one direction. If an object is moving in a straight line, speed and velocity are the same, but if it changes direction but remains at the same speed, velocity will have changed but speed remains the same.

To calculate speed, use the equation $Speed = \dfrac{Distance}{Time}$

This can be more easily remembered as an inverted triangle if it is written: AVERAGE SPEED

Equals

DISTANCE

Divided by

TIME

Likewise:

VELOCITY

Equals

DISTANCE

Divided by

TIME

NEWTON'S THREE LAWS OF MOTION

One: An object remains at rest or in uniform motion in a straight line unless an external force is applied to it.

This follows Galileo's concept of inertia and is often called the law of inertia.

Two: An object's rate of change of momentum is proportional to the force causing it. The relationship between an object's mass, m; its acceleration, a; and the applied force, F, can be expressed as $F = m \times a$. Or more simply summarized, acceleration is directly related to the force applied.

This is the most powerful of the three laws.

Three: For every action there is an equal and opposite reaction.

This law basically explains what happens if we step off a moving train onto the stationary platform.

As an aid to remembering them, think of the first as one (I) ertia, and the third as an upside down 3, which can be seen as "equal and opposite."

SIR ISAAC NEWTON

Isaac Newton was a physicist, mathematician, astronomer, theologian, alchemist and natural philosopher, and the greatest scientist of his age. He was born on January 4, 1643, in Woolsthorpe, Lincolnshire. It was at Cambridge University that he became interested in mathematics, physics, astronomy, and optics, but the plague forced the university to close in October 1665 and he returned home. He later described the two years 1665 and 1666 as the "prime of my age for invention." It was at this time that he began to think about gravity and to develop his ideas on calculus.

In 1667, Newton returned to Cambridge, where he became a fellow of Trinity College and was later appointed second Lucasian professor of mathematics. From the mid-1660s Newton conducted experiments on the composition of light, discovering that white light is composed of the same colors as the rainbow. It was this work, particularly after the development of his reflecting telescope in 1668, that captured the attention of the scientific world, and he was made a Fellow of the Royal Society in 1672. In 1704 he published *The Opticks*, which outlined his discoveries on light and color and established the modern study of the behavior of light.

Newton published widely, his most famous single work being the *Philosophia Naturalis Principia Mathematica* (Mathematical Principles of Natural Philosophy), published in 1687 with the help of the astronomer Edmond Halley. In it he described universal gravitation, how a universal force such as gravity applied to all objects in all parts of the universe, as well as the three laws of motion. He demonstrated the consistency between Kepler's laws of planetary motion and his theory of gravity. His findings removed the last doubts about heliocentrism and advanced the scientific revolution. These principles were to dominate the scientific view of the universe for the next three centuries.

In 1689 Newton became a member of Parliament for Cambridge University and was appointed warden of the Royal Mint in 1696. He was knighted in 1705 and elected president of the Royal Society, an office he held until his death in 1727. He is buried in Westminster Abbey.

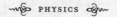

COLOR BANDS ON RESISTORS

There are several versions of mnemonic sentences to help remember the color codes of resistors, capacitors, and other electronic components. Most are very un-PC. Here are two more acceptable examples:

Billy Brown Revives On Your Gin But Values Good Whiskey.

Black, Brown, Red, Orange, Yellow, Green, Blue, Violet, Gray, White, and if you want to add Gold or Silver tolerance:

Betty Brown Races Over Your Gran But Violet Generally Wins Gold or Silver.

ASTRONOMY

*"Astronomy compels the soul to look upwards
and leads us from this world to another."*

PLATO

L ike many people, I had the order of the planets in the solar system fixed firmly in my mind through the mnemonic "My Very Educated Mother Just Served Us Nine Pies," along with a suitable revision when Pluto was demoted. However, until I began researching this book I had no idea how many alternative versions of the mnemonic there were, nor just how many others existed for anything to do with the stars and planets.

THE PLANETS OF THE SOLAR SYSTEM

There are many versions of mnemonic sentences to place the planets in the correct order in the solar system. Working out from the sun at the center they are:

Mercury, Venus, Earth, Mars, Jupiter, Saturn, Uranus, Neptune, Pluto.

My preferred one is:

My Very Educated Mother Just Served Us Nine Pies.

Of course, you also need to remember that every 248 years Neptune becomes the farthest planet for 20 years, in which case you could end the sentence with "Pine Nuts." This last happened between 1979 and 2000.

And if you want them in reverse:

Plainly, Naughty Uncensored Sex Jokes Make Embarrassed Virgins Mad.

PLANETS IN ORDER OF SIZE

The planets of the solar system in order of mass and equatorial diameter are, largest first:

Jupiter, Saturn, Uranus, Neptune, Earth, Venus, Mars, Mercury, Pluto.

Which can be remembered as:

Jason Sat Under Ninety-Eight Vicious Monster Munching Penguins.

And in ascending order, smallest first:

Pluto Must Meet Venus Every Night Until Saturn Jumps, or *Pop Music Makes Vikings Even Naughtier Until Saxons Jiggle.*

And to distinguish Mars from Mercury:

Pluto's Mercenaries March Valiantly Every Night Up Satan's Jockstrap.

Of course, all of these were devised before the debate over whether or not Pluto is a planet.

> ## *Pluto is not a planet . . .*
> There has also been considerable debate over whether
> Pluto can really be classified as a planet at all. In August
> 2006, the International Astronomical Union ruled that
> the distant ice-covered world is a large example from a
> collection of objects called the Kuiper Belt. It has been
> reclassified as a dwarf planet: just one of more than forty
> discovered so far, including the large asteroid Ceres and
> a very distant object nicknamed Xena, discovered in 2007
> by the astronomer Mike Brown of the California Institute
> at Pasadena.

Correcting the mnemonic after the demotion of Pluto:

My Very Educated Mother Just Served Us Noodles.

And if you want to include the Milky Way Galaxy:

My Very Educated Mother Just Served Us Nuts Mixed With Grapes.

However, that's not the end of the story. Under a planet
definition supported by Mark Sykes, director of the Planetary
Science Institute, if an object is massive enough to be round
and orbit a star, then it should be classified as a planet.

This means that Pluto would be reinstated and would also
add:

Ceres—now identified as the smallest dwarf planet, formerly the first and largest asteroid to be discovered. It was

found by Guisseppe Piazzi in 1801 and orbits between Mars and Jupiter. Ceres may have an ocean of liquid water beneath the surface, making life a possibility;

Charon—now a dwarf planet, but formerly the largest of Pluto's moons;

Makemake—officially named in July 2008, previously nick-named Xena, Makemake orbits beyond Pluto;

Eris—discovered in January 2005 by a Palomar Observatory–based team led by Mike Brown, Eris is the largest dwarf planet;

Haumea—named after a Hawaiian goddess, the dwarf planet, nicknamed Santa, was officially named in September 2008.

This would make the order of the official planets and minor planets of the solar system:

Mercury
Venus
Earth
Mars
Ceres
Jupiter
Saturn
Uranus
Neptune
Pluto
Eris
Makemake
Haumea

And the mnemonic:

My Very Exciting Moment Cementing Justice, Sweetly Usurped Naughty People Cleverly Evading Mainstream Honor.

THE MOONS OF JUPITER

Amalthea, Io, Europa, Ganymede, Callisto:

An Icecube Ever Grows Colder.

And if we leave out Amalthea and concentrate on the four major Galilean moons:

Il Est Grand, Charles.

Jupiter's Moons

Galileo Galilei first discovered Jupiter's four major moons in 1610, using a 20-power telescope; of the four, Ganymede is the largest, followed by Callisto. Additional moons were discovered from the end of the nineteenth century, and there are now sixty-three others known to astronomers, with probably more as yet unfound. All have been given the names of daughters, lovers, and conquests of the Roman god Jupiter or his Greek equivalent, Zeus.

NEPTUNE'S MOONS

Naiad, Thalasso, Despina, Galatea, Larissa, Proteus, Triton, Nereid:

Neptune's Tiny Dancing Girls Look Pretty Tonight.

Neptune has eight moons as well as rings probably made of rocks and dust, unlike Saturn's bright rings made of ice.

The largest is Triton, discovered in 1846 by the English astronomer William Lassell just days after Neptune itself was sighted by a Berlin observatory. Triton is ice covered, with geysers shooting ice five miles into the thin atmosphere. Its surface reflects so much of the little sunlight that reaches it that it is one of the coldest objects in the solar system, with temperatures around $-240°C$ ($-400°F$). There may be water beneath the ice, making some form of life possible, and the moon's center is almost certainly geologically active.

Neptune's other moons are far smaller. Nereid was discovered in 1949, while Naiad, Thalasso, Despina, Galatea, Larissa, and Proteus were located by *Voyager 2* in 1989. As Neptune was the Roman god of the sea, its moons are named after Roman and Greek nymphs and sea gods. Five more small moons were found between 2002 and 2003, none of which have so far been officially named.

SATURN'S MOONS

Mimas, Enceladus, Tethys, Dione, Rhea, Titan, Hyperion, Iapetus, Phoebe.

Which form the acronym:

MET DR. THIP

Although "Thip" is an unlikely name, it is oddly unforgettable.

Saturn's nine moons were all discovered before 1900. The largest, Titan, was found in 1655 by Christian Huygens; then Tethys, Dione, Rhea, and Iapetus between 1671 and 1684 by Gian Domenico Cassini; Mimas and Enceladus in 1789 by William Herschel; and Hyperion by W. C. Bond, G. P. Bond, and William Lassell. All were discovered using optical telescopes. With the invention of long-exposure photographic plates, it became possible to discover additional moons, and Phoebe was found in 1899 by W. H. Pickering.

Saturn is now known to have sixty-one moons with confirmed orbits, fifty-three of which have names. The thirty-eight smaller irregular satellites, whose orbits are farther from Saturn, are classified into groups with names from Gallic, Norse, and Inuit mythologies. The twenty-three regular satellites have traditionally been given the names of Titans or other mythological figures associated with Saturn.

Saturn Facts

- Saturn is the second largest planet in the solar system (Jupiter is the largest).
- At its equator, Saturn's diameter is 74,600 miles, almost ten times the diameter of Earth.
- It was named after the Roman god of agriculture.
- Although the planet can be seen from Earth without a telescope, its seven rings cannot.
- Saturn has a solid inner core but its surface is gas.
- Its atmosphere is mainly hydrogen and helium.
- It has the lowest density of all the planets and is so light it would float if there were an ocean large enough.
- An object weighing 100 pounds on Earth would weigh 116 pounds on Saturn.
- It takes more than twenty-nine years for Saturn to orbit the sun.
- Titan is the only one of Saturn's moons to have an atmosphere.
- Titan is actually larger than the planet Mercury.
- Titan's atmosphere is so dense that it is only recently that astronomers have begun to see its surface. They have discovered lakes of liquid methane and ethane near the poles and clouds in the atmosphere.
- Recent images from the *Cassini* spacecraft suggest that Titan has geological features that are similar to Earth's.

- A giant crater on the surface of Mimas makes it resemble the "Death Star" in *Star Wars*.
- Iapetus is dark on one side and very bright on the other.
- Pandora and Prometheus are dubbed the shepherd moons because they herd particles into Saturn's "F" ring.
- Phoebe is extremely dark, with an unusual orbit that leads astronomers to think is may be an asteroid or object from the Kuiper Belt that was caught by Saturn's strong gravitational pull aeons ago.

Enceladus

In June 2009 scientists reported that Enceladus, a tiny moon of Saturn, could be one of the most promising places in the solar system to search for extraterrestrial life.

A probe from NASA's *Cassini* spacecraft has detected ice crystals of sodium salts that seem to come from plumes emanating from the south pole. These are similar to those found in our own oceans and support scientists' belief that there may be liquid water in caverns beneath the icy surface of Enceladus.

"We need three ingredients for life, as far as we know—liquid water, energy, and the basic chemical building blocks—and we seem to have all three at Enceladus," said John Spencer, a *Cassini* scientist from Southwest Research Institute, Boulder, Colorado.

THE MOON

Have you ever looked at a sliver of silver moon and wondered whether it was waxing or waning? Just think:

When **C**oming, the moon is really departing.
When **D**eparting, it is really coming.

Or put another way:

A l**E**ft-hand curve to the crescent means the moon is waning or d**E**creasing.
A r**I**ght-hand curve to the crescent means it is waxing or **I**ncreasing.

And:

DOC

D = Waxing.
O = Full.
C = Waning, so when the moon's coming, it's actually going.

STELLAR CLASSIFICATION

The ordered system for classifying stars was originally developed by Annie Jump Cannon (1863–1941). It is sometimes called a "temperature sequence" because it links the spectrum of each star to its surface temperature.

Starting with the hottest, stars are classified in descending order as:

The expression "once in a blue moon" comes about because, not surprisingly, blue moons are rare—well, they happen once every two and a half years. Blue moons are not blue; it just means there have been two full moons in the same calendar month.

A harvest moon refers to the full moon closest to the autumn equinox, when the moon rises for several nights at about the same time as sunset. They were beloved by farmers because they gave precious extra light at harvest time, enabling farmers to carry on working after the sun went down.

A hunter's moon is the first full moon after harvest moon, which coincided with the start of the hunting season.

O, B, A, F, G, K, M.

Which has led to the very well-known astronomical mnemonic:

Oh Be A Fine Girl, Kiss Me.

Or sometimes:

Only Boys Advocating Feminism Get Kissed Meaningfully.

Our sun is a class G in this spectral class system, and depending on their size and composition, stars can also be classified as:

R, N, S (which can be added to the first mnemonic as *Right Now Sweetie*), and C, L, T (which can be remembered as *Research Needs Support. Clever Loving's Tender*).

The classifications R, N, S, and C are given to stars with high carbon content; L and T to stars that are so small they do not generate enough heat to begin nuclear fusion.

REMEMBERING
NAMES AND FACES

"I cannot tell what the dickens his name is."

WILLIAM SHAKESPEARE,
The Merry Wives of Windsor

Many people confess they are terrible at remembering names and faces. In actual fact, they remember the face perfectly well and quite possibly where they met the person; it's the name that eludes them.

Facial recognition is a key part of human perception. The youngest newborn baby quickly learns to recognize its mother's face and soon adds those of other relations and close family friends to this memory store. There have been a number of scientific studies in which groups were shown photographs of faces and other objects and then tested to see what they remembered, hours and days later. In all cases, faces were always by far the most easily recalled.

It seems such a natural thing to do to recognize a face, but think about it for a moment. Most of us recognize thousands of faces: there are the faces of people we know well and those of acquaintances, but we add to these all those people we just see regularly or even occasionally. There are faces we recognize from the train or bus, from college, work, the bank, the supermarket, all people we have maybe never even spoken to, but we know their faces. Then there are actors, film stars, news anchors, celebrities whose faces appear on television and in magazines and newspapers. We recognize and remember them all even after a gap of years and usually know their names, too, depending on how interested we are. We also recognize their different expressions and fairly successfully work out what these mean.

Recognizing faces and expressions is a cognitively complex task. First the brain has to identify a face, next determine whether it is familiar or not, and finally interpret the expression, encoded in the arrangement of eyes and mouth. In the 1990s, scientists narrowed the brain's ability to recognize faces to a region called the fusiform face area, or FFA, located near the back of the brain on the bottom surface, within the fusiform gyrus in the temporal lobe. Magnetic resonance imaging shows this is in a slightly different position for each person and suggests there is also a "place processor" close to the "face processor."

A number of experiments are ongoing to reveal exactly how our brain recognizes and perceives faces. Interestingly, scientists have found that if photographs of famous faces are turned upside down, most people have difficulty recognizing them. In one study, the eyes and eyebrows were inverted; when the pictures were the right way up, everyone spotted the mistake instantly. Not surprisingly, it looked extremely odd, but in the upside-down photos, the error was not obvious at all. However, the ability of face-blind people to recognize faces actually improves if the faces are upside down. Face blindness, or prosopagnosia, is the inability to recognize faces and can be inherited in rare cases, or the result of an injury or disease affecting the face-recognition region of the brain.

If recognizing faces is not the problem, how do we improve our ability to remember names and, more important, match the right name to the face? A person's name is important to them. We are all programmed to react to our own name. How many times have you looked up when you heard your name called, even when you knew it was not you who was being addressed? It's a natural response. So it follows that by using someone's name you will immediately please them and make them feel important. One of the problems is that names usually have no connection to faces. In the past this was often not the case, and surnames at least tended to be associated with professions or jobs, like Thatcher or Cooper, or a physical feature, such as Redhead. Creating an association or connection for yourself is just one of the practical steps you can take to improve your memory for names.

TEN TIPS FOR REMEMBERING NAMES AND FACES

Be interested. Make a conscious decision to take your time when introduced to someone for the first time.

Listen to the name. This sounds obvious but often we are so caught up in what we are going to say that we don't really hear the name in the first place and it's not surprising that we can't remember it later.

Repeat the name immediately. You can do this quite casually to verify that you heard the name correctly, or to check whether the person prefers a shortened or lengthened version of the name. Repeat the name to yourself and again aloud on parting. If you're meeting several people at the same time, there's no shame in requesting a repetition immediately to make sure you know who's who.

Repetition is particularly important if it's an unfamiliar name, and in that case it's worth repeating it several times in your head, breaking it into syllables and really exaggerating the sounds to fix them in your memory.

Really look at the person's face. We know our brains are good at remembering faces, so mentally reconstruct the face in your mind, making a note of any unusual or distinctive feature; it could be something you particularly like or even dislike. Create a cartoon version but make sure you can hear the person's name as you picture it. You can also add any other nonvisual features that stand out, such as a strong accent.

Face association. If you know another person, or someone famous with the same name, picture that person's face alongside this new person. Forge a connection.

Make a mind picture of the name. Turn the name into a picture. It could be something simple like a person "bobbing" up and down behind a wall for Bob, or an image for the whole name. For instance, Sandra Rowe could become an egg timer filled with sand with little arms frantically rowing a boat across a choppy lake. The more colorful or bizarre the image, the more likely it is to stick.

Imagine writing the name in different scripts and colors, saying it aloud to yourself as you write. Really visualize the name and ask to clarify the spelling if it is at all unusual. People won't mind, it shows you are really interested.

Franklin D. Roosevelt seemed to remember the names of virtually everyone he met effortlessly. Apparently, he used to imagine the person's name written across their forehead. You could develop this by changing the calligraphy or design depending upon the sort of person they are; the name could be engraved in wood, jeweled, plain, colorful, or even embroidered on an appropriate hat. Paris Hilton could wear a jeweled tiara of her name, someone called Alice could wear an Alice band or, if you prefer rhymes, a palace-shaped hat. The possibilities are endless, just use your imagination and have fun.

Exchange cards, especially in a business setting. The Japanese consider card exchange a major social function, just as the Victorians and Edwardians used to leave calling cards. If you've met someone in an official capacity, write down their name and where you met them in a notebook or computer file for future reference when needed.

Trust yourself. Stop making excuses or telling yourself you are dreadful at remembering names and instead just concentrate.

GEOGRAPHY

"Many complain of their memory,
few of their judgment."

BENJAMIN FRANKLIN

Geographical mnemonics such as the ones for stalagmites and -tites, latitude and longitude, the tropics, great lakes and oceans were all long ago firmly fixed in my memory. Others, like the song "Fifty Nifty United States," were a real revelation and they obviously work: I found a clip of a four-year-old girl who could sing her way through the states perfectly, although she could barely pronounce some of the names.

OCEANS

The four oceans of the world—Indian, Arctic, Atlantic, and Pacific—can be remembered by:

I Am A Person.

THE SEVEN CONTINENTS

Eat An Aspirin After A Nighttime Snack, or
SEAN got three AAAs!

are mnemonics for the seven continents. The second letter in the first three A words helps to recall the A continents:

Europe, Antarctica, Asia, Africa, Australia, North America, South America.

In order of size, beginning with the smallest, they are:

Australia
Europe
Antarctica
South America
North America
Africa
Asia

Audrey Excites Another Sailor. Nothing Affects Alistair.

COMPASS POINTS

To remember directions, use the sentence:

Never Eat Shredded Wheat, or
Never Eat Soggy Wafers.

Think of a clock face and place the first letter of each word under the 12, 3, 6, and 9 beginning with N at 12 o'clock.

LONGITUDE AND LATITUDE

LONGitude is the distance aLONG the equator starting from 0° at Greenwich or the prime meridian in London.

LATitude is the lateral or sideways distance in degrees

north or south from the equator, which is zero degrees latitude.

It also helps to think of longitude as long, which always sounds vertical or tall.

THE EQUATOR AND THE TROPICS

CaNcer lies North of the equator
And CapricOrn lies Opposite, or south.

More simply, just remember cancer tends to affect the chest and corns are found on feet, so Capricorn lies below Cancer.

The equator is the longest line of latitude at 248,595.179 miles long and it divides Earth into the northern and southern hemispheres. The sun is directly overhead on the equator at noon on the two equinoxes around March 21 and September 23. It runs through Indonesia, Ecuador, Brazil, the Democratic Republic of the Congo, and Kenya.

The tropics of Cancer and Capricorn mark the lines where the sun is directly overhead at noon on the two solstices: the tropic of Cancer on June 21 marking the beginning of summer in the northern hemisphere and winter in the southern; and the tropic of Capricorn on December 21 marking the start of summer in the southern hemisphere and winter in the northern.

The tropic of Cancer lies at 23.5° latitude north of the equator. Beginning at the Greenwich or prime meridian at zero degrees longitude heading eastward, the tropic of Cancer runs through Algeria, Niger, Libya, Egypt, the Red Sea, Saudi Arabia, United Arab Emirates, Oman, the Indian Ocean, India, Bangladesh, Burma, China, the Taiwan Strait, the Republic of China, the Pacific Ocean, Hawaii (the sea area only), Mexico, Gulfs of California, Mexico, and Straits of Florida, the Bahamas, Atlantic Ocean, Western Sahara, Mauritania, Mali, Algeria.

The tropic of Capricorn lies at 23.5° latitude south of the equator and runs through Australia, Chile, southern Brazil (which is the only country that is crossed by both the equator and a tropic), Namibia, Madagascar, and Mozambique. Beginning at zero degrees longitude and moving eastward, the tropic of Capricorn passes through the Atlantic Ocean, Namibia, Botswana, South Africa, Mozambique, the Indian Ocean, Madagascar, the Indian Ocean, Australia, the Pacific Ocean, Chile, Argentina, Paraguay, Brazil, the Atlantic Ocean. The positions of both tropics are not actually fixed but can vary over time depending on the tilt of Earth's axis relative to the plane of its orbit around the sun. Latitudes above the tropic of Cancer are known as the northern temperate zone and south of the tropic of Capricorn as the southern temperate zone.

THE WORLD'S LONGEST RIVERS

There can be differences of opinion on this according to the determination of the river's course and its tributaries, but this acronym is still useful:

NAMMI YACH-Y

Nile (Africa), 4,145 miles
Amazon (South America), 3,977 miles, although the
    largest by volume
Mississippi and Missouri, as a combined river system
    (USA)
Irtysh (Russia)
Yangtse (China)
Amur (Asia)
Congo (Africa)
Huang, or Yellow (China)

NORTH AFRICA

The countries of North Africa from west to east are:

Morocco, Algeria, Tunisia, Libya, Egypt.

Many African Tourists Like Elephants is a neat reminder.

THE UNITED STATES OF AMERICA

The Fifty States

To remember the number of states, think of the song title by Ray Charles: "Fifty Nifty United States," which, if you know the lyrics, too, lists each by name. To hear the whole song, simply go to YouTube and pick your preferred version.

Here are the words:

Fifty Nifty United States from thirteen original colonies;
Fifty Nifty stars on the flag that billows so beautifully in the breeze.
Each individual state contributes a quality that is great.
Each individual state deserves a bow, we salute them now.

Fifty Nifty United States from thirteen original colonies,
Shout 'em, scout 'em, tell all about 'em,
One by one, till we've given a day to every state in the USA.
Alabama, Alaska, Arizona, Arkansas, California, Colorado, Connecticut,
Delaware, Florida, Georgia, Hawaii, Idaho, Illinois, Indiana.
Iowa, Kansas, Kentucky, Louisiana, Maine,
Maryland, Massachusetts, Michigan,
Minnesota, Mississippi, Missouri, Montana,
Nebraska, Nevada,
New Hampshire, New Jersey, New Mexico, New York,
North Carolina, North Dakota, Ohio,
Oklahoma, Oregon, Pennsylvania, Rhode Island, South Carolina,

South Dakota, Tennessee, Texas,
Utah, Vermont, Virginia, Washington, West Virginia,
Wisconsin, Wyoming.

North, South, East, West in a calm, objective opinion (*choose
your favorite State*)
Is the Best of the Fifty Nifty United States from thirteen
original colonies.
Shout 'em, scout 'em, tell all about 'em
One by One, till we've given a day to every state in the good
old U . . . S . . . A.

I was surprised by how much there is in the same vein, so if the idea appeals, check out Animaniacs' video of Wakko's 50 State Capitals and Presidents; and also Yakko's Nations of the World and Universe Song, to name just a few.

And working on the principle that it's far easier to remember which state you have forgotten if you at least know what letter it begins with, this nonsense sentence is helpful—just ignore all the "Es" and remember not to add a "b" to *numb*!

*Evening Arctic snow can num mammoth Mike's lip, knee,
and even me. Few ewe mow me.*

The States Next to California

To be sure which states border California:

On top is	Oregon
Next to	Nevada
Also next to	Arizona
Much down	Mexico
Precisely west	Pacific Ocean

The Great Lakes

The Great Lakes—Huron, Ontario, Michigan, Erie, and Superior—can be easily remembered because the first letter of each spells

HOMES.

Sam's Horse Must Eat Oats recalls them in order of size, and to geographically place them from west to east:

Sally Made Henry Eat Oreos.

CENTRAL AMERICA

The countries of Central America are:

Mexico, Guatemala, Belize, El Salvador, Honduras, Nicaragua, Costa Rica, Panama, which can be more easily brought to mind by:

My Goodness But Eating Hot Nachos Causes Pain.

Alternatively, you could exclude Mexico and remind yourself

of the Central American countries south of the border in several sentences:

Beatrice, Give Every Hungry Nerd Cocoa Puffs.
Big Gorillas Eat Hotdogs Not Cold Pizza.
Big Grandmother Earned Her Nickels Cooking Pies.
Big George Earned His Noodles Causing Pain.

LAND BIOMES

Biomes are the world's major habitats. They are specialized ecosystems defined by their environment: factors like temperature, rainfall, altitude, and latitude, and by the animals and vegetation found in them.

There are six major land biomes:

Tundras
Deciduous forests
Deserts
Grasslands
Tropical rain forests
Coniferous forests

They can be remembered by:

The Dry Desert Grows Terrific Castles.

STALACTITES AND STALAGMITES

There are several mnemonics to distinguish between the two:

> *Stala**c**tites point from **c**eiling downward, and*
> *Stala**g**mites point **g**round upward.*

Or:

> *Stala**ctites** cling **tight**,*
> *Stala**gmites** grow **mighty**.*

I have to say I find it easier to just think,

> *Tights fall down, while mites crawl on the ground.*

Stalactites and stalagmites form in pairs in limestone caves, due to water dripping and evaporating, leaving behind deposits of calcium carbonate dissolved from rock that build up over thousands of years. Stalactites tend to be long and thin, looking something like icicles. Stalagmites form directly below as the water falls to the floor and the resulting splash means they are usually shorter and thicker than stalactites. Eventually the two meet to form a single column.

GEOLOGICAL TIME PERIODS

Ever wondered which came first, the Jurassic or the Cretaceous, or when exactly the Cambrian was? Just remember:

Pregnant Camels Often Sit Down Carefully. Perhaps Their Joints Creak?

This should help you get the correct order for each Period: Pre-Cambrian, Ordovician, Silurian, Devonian, Carboniferous, Permian, Triassic, Jurassic, Cretaceous.

To add the more recent epochs to these, remember:

Possibly Early Oiling Might Prevent Painful Rheumatism.

Paleocene, Eocene, Oligocene, Miocene, Pliocene, Pleistocene, Recent.

Or you could use:

Possibly Early Oiling Might Prevent Premature Hollowing

if you prefer to include Holocene rather than Recent.

Periods & Epochs	Million Years Ago	Key Events
Pre-Cambrian	up to 544	Land masses begin to break up. Algae and trace fossils.
Cambrian	500–440	Major diversification in the Cambrian Explosion. First green plants and fungi.
Silurian	440–410	First millipedes and jawed fish, corals, trilobites, and mollusks.
Devonian	410–360	Large primitive trees, early form of sharks.
Carboniferous	360–286	Appearance of winged insects, amphibians, first reptiles, and coal forests.
Permian	286–245	Permian Triassic extinction event destroying 95% of

Periods & Epochs	Million Years Ago	Key Events
		life including trilobites. Mosses and seed plants, beetles, and flies appear.
Triassic	245–208	Dinosaurs dominant on land and sea. Early mammals and primitive crocodiles.
Jurassic	208–146	Conifers and ferns widespread. First birds and lizards appear along with many dinosaurs, including sauropods, carnosaurs, and stegosaurs.
Cretaceous	146–65	Appearance of mammals, flowering plants, new types of insects, ammonites, new types of

Periods & Epochs	Million Years Ago	Key Events
		dinosaurs including tyrannosaurs, modern sharks, and crocodiles.
Tertiary Period	65–1.8	
Paleocene	65–54	Tropical climate. Mammals diversify and first large mammals appear following the extinction of the dinosaurs.
Eocene	54–37	Lowering of CO_2 levels.
Oligocene	38–23	Rapid evolution and diversification of flora and fauna.
Miocene	23–1.8	Recognizable mammal and bird families. First apes, grasses, and forests.
Quaternary Period	1.8–today	

Periods & Epochs	Years Ago	Key Events
Pleistocene	1.8 mil.—11,000	Humans appear.
Recent	11,000—today	Development of human culture, beginning of global warming and climate change.

MOHS' HARDNESS SCALE

The Mohs' scale of mineral hardness groups minerals into ten categories in ascending order according to their relative hardness. It was created by the German mineralogist Friedrich Mohs in 1812 and assesses the scratch resistance of various minerals. This is just one method of defining hardness, but the basic idea seems to have its roots in antiquity. It was mentioned by Theophrastus around 300 BC and Pliny the Elder in *Naturalis Historia* around 77 BC.

The minerals in each group are capable of scratching those in the preceding group.

The Mohs' Scale

1	Talc or mica	Used in talcum powder.
2	Gypsum or rock salt	Formed when seawater evaporates. Used in plaster of Paris.
3	Calcite	Limestone and many shells contain calcite.
4	Fluorite	Fluorine to prevent tooth decay is found in fluorite.
5	Apatite	A group of phosphate minerals. Hydroxylapatite is the major component of tooth enamel.
6	Orthaclase	Also known as feldspar, the most abundant mineral in Earth's continental crust.
7	Quartz	Second most abundant mineral after feldspar.
8	Topaz	Pure topaz is colorless and transparent, but it is usually tinted with impurities.
9	Corundum	Rubies and sapphires are corundums. Twice as hard as topaz.
10	Diamond	Prized in jewelry, also used in cutting tools. Four times as hard as corundum.

Groups 1 and 2 can be scratched by a fingernail, 3 to 6 by a knife, and groups 7–10 are hard enough to scratch glass. There are also some everyday items that can fit into the scale:

A fingernail is 2.5, a knife blade and glass are 5.5, and a steel file is 6.5.

There are several mnemonic sentences to remember each group:

Toronto Girls Can Flirt And Only Quit To Chase Dwarves.

Terrible Giants Can Find Alligators Or Quaint Tigers Conveniently Digestible.

True Geologists Climb Faults And Observe Quarries To Contemplate Deformation.

HOW DO ACTORS LEARN LINES?

*"Learning is not attained by chance,
it must be sought for with ardour and attended
to with diligence."*

ABIGAIL ADAMS

To most outside the theatrical profession, learning lines seems one of the most difficult tasks facing an actor, involving endless hours spent poring over their part in an effort to memorize the script. In fact, that is not the way most actors work, and it is certainly not the most effective way to learn.

In a Columbia University discussion on memory, Michael Boyd, the artistic director of the Royal Shakespeare Company (RSC), and Oliver Sacks, professor of neurology and psychiatry at Columbia University Medical Center, looked at the idea of learning lines and memory being more than just a mental process. Boyd worked with some thirty actors over a period of three years on the RSC's last complete cycle of Shakespeare's history plays. All of the actors were involved in at least seven plays, with a vast number of roles and lines to learn. Several of the plays were not worked on at all for almost a year, and when they returned to them, all the actors were very concerned that they would have forgotten their lines. And indeed it seemed they had. Working alone and during a line-run recall was generally poor. It wasn't until they stood on stage and began acting, even without costumes, props, and scenery, that the actors remembered their parts. In fact, they remembered so well they were almost immediately word perfect. They were even better when there was an audience.

It seemed the memory of the lines was still there, but it needed unlocking by a combination of body movement and, most important, emotion. Increasingly, evidence suggests that memory is not just a mental process but something that involves the whole body. Michael Boyd went on to cite a neurobiological study of London taxi drivers that showed their hippocampi (the parts of the brain involved in memory) were enlarged after they had taken the test known as the Knowledge. More relevant to his work with actors, though, taxi drivers remembered locations only if they physicalized their memory; their sense of location was dependent upon their having a physical sense of turning left or right.

This experience with the actors was in line with Oliver Sacks's work with the musician Clive Wearing, whose hippocampus had been damaged by encephalitis some twenty years earlier. Wearing's memory lasted just seven seconds, but he was still able to conduct, play the piano, and sing complex musical works. When asked about a piece of music, he seemed to remember nothing, but when his hands were on the piano, he could play perfectly. Similarly, there are cases of actors suffering from Alzheimer's who can still act out lengthy roles.

Increasingly, scientists believe that memory is a physical and emotional response. One of the key elements in most memory techniques is forging a connection to create an emotional response or link with the material you are trying to learn.

A 2006 study by Helga and Tony Noice published in the *Journal of the Association for Psychological Science* comes to the same conclusions. Helga Noice is a cognitive psychologist at Elmhurst College and Tony Noice a cognitive researcher, actor, and director at Indiana State University; they spent two decades making a psychological study of actors.

They found the secret of actors' abilities to learn lines is basically acting. Put more simply, when learning, actors really concentrate on the meaning of lines, their physical and emotional aspects, all the time considering ways to communicate meaning to others.

Crucially, actors break the script into a series of chunks, often called "beats," which contain a single immediate intention as a reaction to another character. They keep asking "why?" in order to understand a character's overall plan and intention, particularly in relation to other characters. In this way a script becomes a series of beats, each logically linked with the next.

Michael Caine explains, "You must be able to stand there not thinking of that line. You take it off the other actor's face."

The Noices call this "active experiencing," channeling emotions, movement, and mental powers to communicate meaning. This is definitely a way of learning that can be usefully employed by nonactors. Studies have found that students who imagine explaining and conveying material to other people when they learn retain more information than those who learn by rote.

The Noices also studied the effects of their "active

239

experience" principle of learning on a group of older people who took part in a four-week acting course. Afterward the group showed significant improvements in word recall, problem-solving, and memory retention, with the improvements more marked after a four-month gap.

Other researchers on memory have come to similar conclusions, suggesting that memory relies on emotion, action, and understanding.

KEY TIPS FOR LEARNING LINES

· Memorizing anything takes time and you do need to make an effort.

· Really look at the words and make sure you understand.

· Say the words aloud.

· Learn lines in context. Experts emphasize "gist" learning—understanding the meaning behind the words, the motivations, and overall intentions.

· Look at the whole, then divide and subdivide right down to sentences. Really think and make sure you understand.

· One of the keys to learning is organization and the ability to retrieve a memory.

· Break material into manageable chunks containing a single intention or idea.

· Establish logical links between each chunk or beat.

- Look for patterns. Pick out the most important words and look for the relationship between them.
- Some people favor cue or flash cards.
- Coupling information with emotions or imagining a physical action helps fix the memory.
- Retype your lines. It's amazing how much you will have retained afterward.
- Play with what you're learning. Try handwriting a line, but only write the first letter of each word.
- Tape recordings can really help, especially if you are an auditory person. They're also useful if you drive a lot because you can play them in the car. Start with your own part but then just record others' lines as a prompt for your own.
- Take time away from the material to give your brain a chance to process and store.

WEATHER

*"Sunshine is delicious, rain is refreshing,
wind braces up, snow is exhilarating; there is
no such thing as bad weather, only different
kinds of good weather."*

JOHN RUSKIN

There are many verses and sayings about the weather, most of which have become part of our folklore and seem to be assimilated rather than consciously learned. When most were composed and by whom remains unknown, but they act as general mnemonics, helping us predict and understand our weather.

RAINBOWS

The seven colors of the rainbow (or color spectrum) have given us one of the most famous mnemonics of all:

Richard Of York Gave Battle In Vain.

Red, Orange, Yellow, Green, Blue, Indigo, Violet.

The sentence is a reference to Richard III, more particularly as portrayed in Shakespeare's eponymous play. Variations have been composed, but why meddle with something that has worked well for so long?

SKIES AND RAINBOWS

Red sky at night,
Shepherds' delight.
Red sky in the morning,
Shepherds' warning.

This is one of the oldest weather sayings and sometimes includes sailors rather than shepherds, which makes sense because predicting the weather is obviously very important to both.

The rhyme was probably passed on by word of mouth long before it was ever written down, but to give an indication of how ancient it is, in the New Testament, Matthew 16:2–3 says, "When it is evening, you say, 'It will be fair, for the sky is red.' And in the morning, 'It will be stormy today, for the sky is red and threatening.' You know how to interpret the appearance of the sky."

The saying is also referenced in Shakespeare, in a line from *Venus and Adonis*, published in 1593: "Like a red morn that ever yet betoken'd wreck to the seaman—sorrow to shepherds."

It does make meteorological sense. Sunlight travels through more atmosphere when it is low in the sky, at dawn and dusk. The red/orange part of the spectrum of light keeps a more direct course and is better reflected back from clouds. If there is broken cloud in the morning approaching from the west and possibly bringing rain, we are more likely to see red light reflecting back from the cloud. Red clouds at dusk suggest that any storm clouds have passed, giving a good chance of clear skies ahead.

> *Rainbow in the morning,*
> *Travelers take warning.*
> *Rainbow at night,*
> *Travelers' delight.*

This also has a logical explanation. Rainbows indicate humid air, and as a morning rainbow would be seen in the west, the direction from which storms generally come in the United Kingdom because the wind is primarily westerly, they often appear before bad weather. On the other hand, evening rainbows that appear in the east often indicate the passing of stormy weather.

> *Morning red, evening gray,*
> *Two sure signs of one fine day.*

GOOD AND BAD WEATHER

Low pressure forces smoke down:

> *When smoke descends, good weather ends.*

> *When smoke hovers close to the ground,*
> *There will be a weather change.*

> *When down the chimney falls the soot,*
> *Mud will soon be underfoot.*

In fine weather, sound waves travel upward and outward in the atmosphere, whereas on humid, cloudy days they are sent back to the ground:

> *Sound traveling far and wide*
> *A stormy day this doth betide.*

And along the same lines:

> *When forests murmur and mountains roar,*
> *Close your windows and shut the door.*
>
> *When ditch and pond offend the nose,*
> *Look out for rain and stormy blows.*

Just as sound travels farther as storms approach, so do smells.

In the northern hemisphere you can find the center of a weather system:

> *When the wind is at your back, the low is on your left.*

This would be reversed in the southern hemisphere.

Pilots use the following mnemonic:

> *High to low:*
> *Look out below.*
> *Low to high:*
> *Clear blue sky.*

This is because if pressure temperature drops, you will be lower in altitude than the aircraft's instruments suggest if they are left uncorrected. Alternatively, a rise in pressure temperature will result in the opposite effect:

When larks fly high, expect fair weather.

From the West Country:

In March and April there be showers,
They go on for hours and hours.
Then comes May, the farmers say,
Frost by night and hail by day.
Then comes June, the sun is hot,
Is it shining? No, it's not.

When March roars in like a lion, it will go out like a lamb.

Seagull, seagull, sit on the sand,
It's never good weather while you're on the land.

When seagulls fly to land,
A storm is at hand.

When the wind is in the east,
'Tis neither good for man nor beast.

TEMPERATURE

Crickets chirp faster as the temperature rises.

Cold is the night
When stars shine bright.

And:

Clear nights, cold days.

As the days begin to shorten,
The heat begins to scorch 'em;
As the days begin to lengthen,
The cold begins to strengthen.

This should be generally true because the hottest of the summer weather and coldest winter weather tend to be after the solstices.

RAIN, RAIN, GO AWAY

Rain before seven, fine before eleven.

The louder the frog, the more rain.

When geese are cackling, here comes rain.

When grass is dry in the morning light,
Look for rain before the night.
When dew is in the grass,
Rain will never come to pass.

This does make sense in that dew forming overnight is a sign of good weather and a cloudless sky, whereas the absence of dew indicates either that it is cloudy or there is a strong breeze, both of which could mean rain.

A wind from the south has rain in its mouth.

If the cows are lying down, rain is on its way.

St. Swithun's Day, if it does rain,
Full forty days it will remain;
St. Swithun's Day, if it be fair,
For forty days 'twill rain no more.

St. Swithun's Day falls on July 15, and although probably dating from the Middle Ages, this rhyme has no basis in fact.

A summer fog for fair,
Winter fog for rain.

Ground fog in summer is usually a sign it's going to be hot and sunny later, whereas winter fog often brings rain.

If a circle forms around the moon,
It's sure to rain, very soon.

Or:

A ring around the sun or moon,
Means rain or snow coming soon.

Circles around the sun or moon are called halos, and they are formed by light refracting, or bending, as it passes through the ice crystals that form in high-level cirrus and cirrostratus clouds. Although these clouds do not themselves produce rain or snow, they often indicate an advancing low pressure system that may do so.

When leaves show their undersides,
Be very sure that rain betides.

When clouds appear like rocks and towers,
The earth's refreshed by frequent showers.

MUSIC

"After silence, that which comes closest to expressing the inexpressible is music."

Aldous Huxley

M nemonics play an important part in the early lessons of everyone who has ever learned to read music or play an instrument.

READING THE NOTES

The notes represented by the five lines on the treble stave from bottom to top are E, G, B, D, F:

> *Every Good Boy Deserves Favors*, or
> *Every Good Boy Deserves Fun*.

The corresponding spaces in the treble clef are F, A, C, E, which spell the easily remembered *face.* Or you may prefer:

> *Fat Angels Crash Easily*.

The order of notes on the lines of the bass clef are G, B, D, F, A:

> *Green Birds Do Fly Away*, or linking with the treble clef,

Good Boys Do Fine, Always, and the version my piano teacher taught me:

Great British Dancers Float Away.

The corresponding spaces of the bass clef are A, C, E, G:

All Cows Eat Grass.

The order for adding sharps is called the circle of fifths, F, C, G, D, A, E, B:

Father Christmas Gets Drunk After Every Beer.
Five Cool Guys Danced Away Every Beat.
Father Charles Goes Down And Ends Battle.

This last mnemonic can be neatly reversed for the order of flats in flat key signatures, B, E, A, D, G, F, C:

Battle Ends And Down Goes Father Charles.

MUSICAL MODES

The order of musical modes

The musical modes as based on the white keys of a piano starting with middle C are Ionian mode, Dorian mode, Phrygian mode, Lydian mode, Mixolydian mode, Aeolian mode, Locrian mode:

I Don't Punch Like Muhammad Al Lee.

GUITAR STRINGS

The strings on a standard tuned guitar beginning with the lowest, heaviest gauge string are E, A, D, G, B, E:

Even After Dinner, Growing Boys Eat, or
Elephants And Donkeys Grow Big Ears.

Or in the reverse order, E, B, G, D, A, E:

Excited Bunnies Get Drunk At Easter.

SPORTS

"Sports do not build character. They reveal it."

HEYWOOD BROUN

Surprisingly, there seem to be very few mnemonics specifically for sports. It may be because the outcome of a game is something that fans feel so passionately about that they don't need mnemonics to help them remember the details. All the key elements necessary for good recall are already there: interest, intense emotion, vivid imagery, and associations, alongside ample opportunity for repetition while talking over and reliving the excitement of the game.

ACRONYMS IN SPORTS

While not the richest source of mnemonics in general, sports do lend themselves to acronyms. Here are just a few of the best known:

NBA	National Basketball Association
NFL	National Football League
AFC	American Football Conference
NFC	National Football Conference
MLB	Major League Baseball
PGA	Professional Golfers' Association

LPGA	Ladies Professional Golf Association
IOC	International Olympic Committee
NASCAR	National Association for Stock Car Auto Racing
WWE	World Wrestling Entertainment
SCUBA	Self-Contained Underwater Breathing Apparatus
HALO	High Altitude, Low Opening (Skydiving)

TEAM AND PLAYER NICKNAMES

The often affectionate and always colorful nicknames given to both teams and players are another type of mnemonic. It's easy to forget a standard name, but it's much harder to forget a nickname. George Herman Ruth, or Babe Ruth, also known as the Sultan of Swat? Nicknames also have the advantage of telling you something about the player. Shoeless Joe Jackson earned his nickname because once in a minor league game he took off a pair of new shoes that were too tight and played in his socks.

Baseball team nicknames have evolved over the years, sometimes connected with color, such as the Boston Red Sox, the Chicago White Sox, and the Cincinnati Reds. They might also reflect something that makes the team or city distinct; so we have the Cleveland Spiders (the team at the time was particularly agile) and the Brooklyn Trolley Dodgers.

Colleges and their teams also have nicknames, with swift or fierce animals particularly popular, so there are a large number of bears, wildcats, tigers, eagles, and hawks as well as pioneers, saints, warriors, and Spartans, reflecting a certain character. Unsurprisingly, there is only one team called the Banana Slugs—the University of California, Santa Cruz—and they are all the more memorable for it.

American football teams are just as imaginatively nicknamed. So there are the Ain'ts (New Orleans Saints), Big Blue (New York Giants), the Skins (Washington Redskins), and the Fins (Miami Dolphins).

SOCCER

Soccer fans may not need much help remembering crucial scores, but lists of results lend themselves to the application of pegword memory techniques and particularly the more advanced Peg and Major systems (see pages 104–7). Many memory experts, including Derren Brown, successfully remember results and teams this way.

Taking World Cup winners from 1930, when the tournament began, gives ample opportunity to practice the technique:

World Cup Winners

Year	Final Teams	Score
1930	Uruguay beat Argentina	4–2
1934	Italy beat Czechoslovakia	2–1
1938	Italy beat Hungary	4–2
1950	Uruguay beat Brazil	2–1
1954	W. Germany beat Hungary	3–2
1958	Brazil beat Sweden	5–2
1962	Brazil beat Czechoslovakia	3–1
1966	England beat W. Germany	4–2
1970	Brazil beat Italy	4–1
1974	W. Germany beat Holland	2–1
1978	Argentina beat Holland	3–1
1982	Italy beat W. Germany	3–1
1986	Argentina beat W. Germany	3–2
1990	Germany beat Argentina	1–0
1994	Brazil beat Italy (on penalties)	3–2
1998	France beat Brazil	3–0
2002	Brazil beat Germany	2–0
2006	Italy beat France (on penalties)	5–3

Applying the Major System to the most recent final, split the year 2006 into 20—n and s/z, which suggests the word *nose*; and 06—s/z and j/g, sh or ch; trickier but it could make *sash*, creating an image to represent the year of a nose wrapped in a scarlet sash announcing nose of the year.

Next the teams and scores. These are most simply reduced to I-5 and F-3, which then make I-l and F-m and could translate to *ill* or *hill* and *farm*. The image by which to remember the whole thing then becomes a farmer with a large scarlet sash–wrapped nose (2006) surveying his farm (France 3) perched precariously on top of a hill (Italy 5).

As another example, taking the 19 for granted, '86 becomes f-sh or *fish*, and the teams and scores, Argentina—A-3 or A-m to give *arm*, and W. Germany—WG-2 or WG-n suggesting *wagon*. So the image would become a fish ('86) driving a wagon (W. Germany 2) of arms (Argentina 3)—these could be either weapons or literally severed arms, which is probably a more bizarre and therefore memorable picture.

The success of applying the mnemonic technique obviously depends on your being completely familiar with the pegs, and you should choose the words and images that seem most obvious and appealing to you. The very effort of thinking so hard about each result should help to lodge it firmly in your brain.

THE RINGS ON THE OLYMPIC FLAG

The five rings are colored: Black, Yellow, Blue, Green, Red.

The initial letters of each form BYBGR, and Olympic records can be set BY jumping BiGgeR distances.

SAILING

Tying a Bowline

The most commonly used mnemonic to remind yourself how to tie a bowline involves a rabbit, or occasionally a fox. Either would work:

> *The rabbit pops up out of his hole, hops around the tree,*
> *and disappears back down into the hole again.*

Translated, the "hole" is a small loop in the standing line leading to the fixed object. Hold the small loop in your hand and pass the free end behind your back (the tree). The rabbit is the free end of the rope, and this comes up out of the loop, passes around the standing line (the tree), and goes back down through the loop. To complete the knot, tighten so that it looks something like a seat. The resulting large loop will not tighten when it is lifted.

I am told this is also very useful for a climbing harness. The following rhyme is supposed to clarify the details:

> *Lay the bight to make a hole*
> *Then under the back and around the pole.*
> *Over the top and through the eye*
> *Cinch it tight and let it lie.*

I am not sure that it helps very much without a clear diagram or, better still, someone demonstrating.

Navigation

To make sure you don't hit the shore when entering a harbor, it's worth remembering the simple line for which side the red light should be on:

Red on right upon return.

GAMES

The Order of Suits in Bridge

Spades
Hearts
Diamonds
Clubs

Just think:

Sally Has Dirty Children.

CLASSICS
AND MYTHOLOGY

*"[Memory is] a man's real possession. . . .
In nothing else is he rich, in nothing else
is he poor."*

ALEXANDER SMITH

This section somehow conjures up images of Molesworth and classrooms of pupils chanting Latin verbs. I've omitted those but instead included just a few examples that interested me.

GREAT PHILOSOPHERS

To remember who came first, or who was influenced by whom, just think of the word:

SPA

Socrates (469–399 BC). Renowned for his contribution to ethics, credited as one of the founders of Western philosophy, although he wrote nothing down.

Plato (428–348 BC). His *Dialogues* are the most comprehensive account of Socrates that we have. His writings have been used to teach a range of subjects, including philosophy, logic, rhetoric, and mathematics.

Aristotle (384–322 BC). A student of Plato and teacher of Alexander the Great.

Plato, together with his mentor Socrates and pupil Aristotle, helped to lay the foundations of Western and natural philosophy, ethics, and science.

ROMAN NUMERALS

1	5	10	50	100	500	1000
I	V	X	L	C	D	M

These sentences help you remember them in order:

I Veered across, Lucy Can't Drink Milk, and
I Value Xylophones Like Cows Dig Milk.

THE SEVEN HILLS OF ROME

The hills are called:

Caelian, Quirinal, Viminal, Esquiline, Capitoline,
Aventine, Palatine.

These can be remembered by the question:

Can Queen Victoria Eat Cold Apple Pie?

The seven hills form the geographical heart of Rome within the ancient city walls. The city was said to have been founded by Romulus on the Palatine Hill.

The emperors' palaces were built on the Palatine Hill, which is where the word *palace* comes from. If Nero really did burn Rome in AD 64, when four-fifths of the city was destroyed, he would have watched the blaze from the Palatine Hill. The ruined courts of the Flavian Palace, together with some mosaic paving and sculptures in the Palatine Museum, are all that remain today.

THE THREE GRACES

The Graces were the goddess daughters of Jupiter in Roman mythology and of Zeus in Greek. They were known in Latin as the Gratiae and in ancient Greek as the Charities. They represent Charm, Beauty, and Creativity and have inspired countless sculptors and painters, famously the sixteenth-century painting by Raphael and nineteenth-century sculpture by Canova.

Their names are Euphrosyne, Aglaia, and Thalmia, prompted by:

EAT, or *You frostily Agreed Terms.*

To remember that they symbolize creativity, beauty, and charm, think of:

CBC, or *Create Beautiful Children*.

THE MUSES

The Muses are the goddesses or spirits who are said to inspire the creation of literature and the arts. At first there were said to be three in Classical Greece, but by 400 BC their number had grown to nine.

There are various stories about their origins, but most appropriately for a book about memory, Hesiod's *Theogeny*, written in the seventh century BC, claims they were the daughters of Zeus and Mnemosyne, the goddess of memory.

Their names are:

Muse	Most Associated With	Symbol
Calliope	Epic poetry	Writing tablet
Euterpe	Music	Flute
Clio	History	Scroll
Terpsichore	Dance	Lyre
Thalia	Comedy	Comic mask
Urania	Astronomy	Globe and compass
Polyhymnia	Choral poetry	Veil
Melpomene	Tragedy	Tragic mask
Erato	Lyric poetry	Seven-stringed lyre or guitar

This mnemonic sentence helps to prompt their names:

Calling Every Classics Teacher That Understands Pollyanna's Mental Error.

SCIENTIFIC SURPRISES

· In April 2007, scientists at Columbia University found that it may be possible for people to have "too much memory." This makes it harder for them to filter out and assimilate information, increasing the time it takes for new short-term memories to be processed and stored.

· University of Adelaide researchers found the time of day at which students study influences their ability to learn. Surprisingly, it seems that our brains learn more effectively in the evening.

· This may be because sleep tends to follow evening study sessions, and increasing evidence suggests the brain needs sleep to record information, playing it back to itself as we slumber.

· Age isn't always a disadvantage when it comes to memory. A *Nature Neuroscience* report shows adults can outperform children in remembering the contextual, more complex details.

MEMORY GAMES

"The memory should be specially taxed in youth, since it is then that it is strongest and most tenacious. But in choosing the things that should be committed to memory the utmost care and forethought must be exercised; as lessons well learnt in youth are never forgotten."

ARTHUR SCHOPENHAUER

Some of my best memories of primary school are from break time, and many of the games we played obsessively again and again are in essence memory games. Here are just a few.

THE CONCENTRATION GAME

As with many good games, it starts with everyone sitting in a circle. Each person has a number that they must remember. First the rhythm is set. Everyone slaps their knees twice then claps their hands twice. This is repeated a few times so that everyone is together, then one person chants:

"Are you ready?" slap slap clap clap. "Are you sure?" slap slap clap clap. "Let's begin," slap slap clap clap.

The person who is number one answers, "One one," followed by someone else's number chosen at random. So it could go, "One one seven seven," slap slap clap clap.

Then person number seven answers by adding another person's number without breaking the rhythm, "Seven seven two two," slap slap clap clap.

If anyone falters, forgets their number, or breaks the rhythm, they are out.

KIM'S GAME

Named after Kipling's eponymous hero, this was always popular at birthday parties, and I particularly liked it because it didn't require any physical effort or skill from me, just an attention to detail. The more you play, the better you get. By the end of the party season there was usually serious competition.

The setup is simple: all you need is a tray upon which a variety of small objects are arranged; between ten and twenty is probably ideal. The player is asked to study the tray carefully for a moment or so, then turns away while one of the objects is taken away. The trick is to remember and identify what's missing. There are variations where more than one object is taken or the tray is rearranged. You can even bluff by not removing anything.

THE TRAY GAME

I think this variation of Kim's game is less fun, but its advantage is that it can be played by several people at the same time. The tray is again set up with ten to twenty small items that everyone studies for a moment. The tray is then covered over and everyone is asked to write down each item they remember as quickly as possible. It's best to set a time limit, and the winner is the person who remembers the most objects the fastest.

PARACHUTE GAME

Everyone forms a circle and carefully looks around to memorize who is there. One person is chosen to go outside, and while they are gone, another person hides beneath the parachute (or blanket). When the person returns, they must guess who is hiding. This works well when children are first getting to know one another, in the early days of a new school year or club, but it can also work as a party game.

MIXED MEMORY

As a variation of one person hiding, two people can also switch places and the person returning to the room must work out who. Or instead of people switching, furniture or objects can be moved.

EYEWITNESS REPORTS

Act out a scene or show a clip to a group. Afterward, ask everyone to write down exactly what they saw, together with details of clothing, what was said, how long everything took. Compare accounts to find out just how reliable eyewitnesses really are.

PICNIC BASKET

This game can take many forms. Sometimes it begins with "I'm going on a picnic and in my basket I have strawberries . . ." The next person continues with "I'm going on a picnic and in my basket I have strawberries and cream." The third person remembers both previous ingredients and adds another of their choosing and so on. The object of the game is to remember each item on the list, adding another when it's your turn. People are out if they forget something, and the winner is the last person to make a mistake.

The game can also start with "I'm going to the supermarket to buy . . ." or "I'm going to visit Grandma and in my bag I have . . ." Items on the list can be themed or as quirky and miscellaneous as you please. If you're keen on winning, it's a good idea to choose something quite dull and forgettable when it's your turn.

FINAL THOUGHTS

"Our memory is like a shop in the window of which is exposed now one, now another photograph of the same person. And as a rule the most recent exhibit remains for some time the only one to be seen."

MARCEL PROUST

I hope that after reading this book, you will find that it is not only the most recent entries to your memory store that can be readily accessed. If nothing else, the collection of mnemonics is intended to remind you of things you once knew but had mislaid in the recesses of your memory, and to introduce others that perhaps you never knew but that you find interesting. Above all, I hope it's made you realize that learning things can be fun, that few people have perfect memories but that we can all remember better. It should have helped highlight your strengths and weaknesses and what works best for you.

There are no real quick fixes. Committing anything to memory always involves some effort, but with the right approach, any work involved should bring satisfying results and be enjoyable.

"The secret of a good memory is attention, and attention to a subject depends upon our interest in it. We rarely forget that which has made a deep impression on our minds."

TRYON EDWARDS

ACKNOWLEDGMENTS

First and foremost I should like to thank all those nameless individuals and groups who originally came up with the many varied mnemonic lines and verses included here. There are also a range of websites and books that have proved invaluable for research, particularly: eudesign.com, mindtools.com, OxfordOnline.com, quotationspage.com, the *Oxford Dictionary of Quotations*, and *Brewer's Dictionary of Phrase and Fable*.

On a personal note, thank you to the publisher who originally suggested the idea for the book and to Jo Caseby for her clear thinking and encouragement just when it was most needed. Also to so many friends and family for their contributions, and to Nicola Taplin and the team at Preface.

While every effort has been made to contact copyright holders, the author and publisher would be grateful for information about any material where they have been unable to trace the source, and would be glad to make amendments in further editions.